RESURRECTING JESUS

RESURRECTING JESUS

The Renewal of New Testament Theology

Yung Suk Kim

CASCADE *Books* · Eugene, Oregon

RESURRECTING JESUS
The Renewal of New Testament Theology

Cascade Books
An Imprint of Wipf and Stock Publishers
199 W. 8th Ave., Suite 3
Eugene, OR 97401

www.wipfandstock.com

ISBN 13: 978-1-4982-1834-4

Cataloguing-in-Publication Data

Kim, Yung Suk

Resurrecting Jesus : the renewal of New Testament theology / Yung Suk Kim.

X + Y p. ; 23 cm. Includes bibliographical references.

ISBN 13: 978-1-4982-1834-4

1. Bible. New Testament—Theology. 2. Jesus Christ—Historicity. I. Title.

BS2397 K25 2015

Manufactured in the U.S.A.   07/24/2015

To Robert L. Brawley,
Albert G. McGaw Professor of New Testament Emeritus,
McCormick Theological Seminary, Chicago, IL

Contents

Acknowledgments

IT IS MY HONOR and pleasure to dedicate this book to my first New Testament teacher, Robert L. Brawley, Albert G. McGaw Professor Emeritus at McCormick Theological Seminary, who introduced me to the biblical world and taught me how to engage the New Testament from various interpretive perspectives. According to him, I am the first MDiv student of his who earned a PhD in New Testament studies and became a professor. I also thank my teachers at Vanderbilt University. Among others, Daniel Patte, Professor Emeritus of New Testament, and Fernando Segovia, Oberlin Graduate Professor of New Testament and Early Christianity, have nurtured me as a scholar, strengthening my academic skills and lenses in biblical studies. Also, I cannot thank enough Larry Welborn, my dear friend and colleague, Professor of New Testament at Fordham University, who read my initial book proposal with necessary input. His incisive wisdom encourages me to continue with my work. My special thanks also go to Robert Wafawanaka, my colleague, Associate Professor of Biblical Studies at the School of Theology of Virginia Union University, who took the pain of reading the entire manuscript to give me critical feedback. I also want to express my heartfelt thanks to John Kinney, my dean at the School of Theology, who has trusted and supported me both as a beloved member of the community and as a scholar.

Above all, nothing would have been possible without my family's love and support. My wife Yong-Jeong's sacrifice and love for the family are beyond comparison. I give a big round of hugs to my daughters, HyeRim, HyeKyung, and HyeIn. In particular, HyeKyung read the entire manuscript and gave me a fresh, loving response.

Preface

THIS BOOK REPRESENTS MY own passion for the study of the New Testament and New Testament theology. The New Testament is both a faith document and historical literature, composed of divergent writings that refer to, and reflect on, the life and work of the historical Jesus. The New Testament can be read as a great source/resource for our faith so that today we can continue to testify to the truth that Jesus embodied at all risk. The New Testament also shows historical pictures of Jesus' ministry and of the Evangelists' through which we may learn of their struggles about testifying to the truth in order that we might be challenged in our living of God's good news in the midst of a chaotic world.

This book argues that a solid New Testament theology can be reconstructed based on a critical study of the historical Jesus, by abandoning a traditional divide between New Testament theology and critical studies of the New Testament. Putting Jesus in the context of first-century Judaism in Palestine, this book will reexamine his life, work, death, and resurrection. All in all, a fundamental question this book asks is, "What can we learn from Jesus and how can we build on the significance of his life and work as we do theology for our day in the here and now?"

In the end, this book aims at giving readers the benefits of the following:

- *A better, clearer understanding about the historical Jesus and the New Testament writings that refer to him*

  Just as the body without the spirit is dead, New Testament theology without the historical Jesus is dead because the former is built on the work of the latter. No matter how many gaps exist between the historical Jesus and the New Testament, New Testament theology needs a solid understanding about the historical Jesus. But at the same time, New Testament theology is not only confined to the historical Jesus because it involves Christ-followers' understanding or experience of Jesus and God.

- *Exploring the significance of Jesus' life, teaching, and death, based not on doctrine but on his work of God in first-century Judaism and Palestine*
  While New Testament theology explores Jesus' identity as a point of departure, its scope is more than Jesus. It is impossible to talk about Jesus without God-talk in first-century Judaism. New Testament theology would be misleading if we do not look at God to whom Jesus points his finger. Indeed, Jesus does the works of God, not his own.

- *Redefining New Testament theology as a process of discerning and engaging the historical Jesus and the New Testament writings*
  As I will redefine New Testament theology, here is a short definition: "New Testament theology involves both what the New Testament says about God, the Messiah, and the world, and how the reader evaluates, engages, or interprets diverse yet divergent texts of the New Testament, including difficult, sexist, and oppressive texts. The reader's task is not merely to discern what is good and acceptable in the New Testament, but also to surface its limitations by examining early Christians' disparate positions about God, the Messiah, and the world."

- *Reshaping the reader's overall landscape of New Testament theology*
  With a new, alternative approach to New Testament theology, we expect to redefine central vocabulary in the New Testament, such as "the righteousness of God" (*dikaiosyne tou theou*), "the faith of Christ" (*pistis christou*), and "the kingdom of God" (*basileia tou theou*). For example, the "righteousness of God" will be redefined as God's righteousness rather than as an individual justification. "Faith of Christ Jesus" will be also redefined as his faithfulness through which he proclaims and embodies God's rule in the here and now. Accordingly, "the kingdom of God" will be redefined as God's rule in the here and now that challenges Rome's rule or any obstacles that occlude the flow of God's justice. In the end, Christians will be redefined as Christ-followers who do the works of God.

1

Introduction

NEW TESTAMENT THEOLOGY SHOULD be reconstructed and renewed with a focus on the work of the historical Jesus, who cannot be domesticated by any Christians, scholars, or organizations. Jesus lived his life to his fullest, only "to testify to the truth" (John 18:37). This book is written out of my concerns about doctrinal New Testament theology in which most books of the New Testament are harmoniously or complementarily read to endorse central church doctrines such as "justification by faith." There must be a new way of doing New Testament theology informed by the work of the historical Jesus.

To help readers better understand the birth and origin of this book, I will briefly state my publication history. Reading against the grain of biblical interpretation, in my first book, *Christ's Body in Corinth: The Politics of a Metaphor,* I challenge the traditional ecclesial reading of "the body of Christ" (*soma christou*) in that the body refers to the church (metaphorical organism) and that unity is more important than diversity in the church.[1] I read "the body of Christ" as Christ's own body re-imagined through the image of his crucifixion. So when Paul says in 1 Cor 12:27, "You are the body of Christ," he must mean that *you,* the Corinthians, *not the church,* constitute Christ's body, which is understood as a metaphor for a way of living.[2] That is, you are to embody Christ, imitating his faith even through

1. Kim, *Christ's Body in Corinth.*
2. Ibid., 65–95.

1

risking one's own life. Christ's faith and his bodily life are the basis for the church according to Paul, and followers of Jesus have to imitate him in their lives. All this suggests that for Paul "the body of Christ" is too important to simply apply to an organism, the church, which is referred to as "the body of Christ" only in later epistles not written by Paul: "Christ is the head of the church (*ekklesia*), *his body*" (Eph 5:22); "for the sake of *his body*, that is, the church (*ekklesia*)" (Col 1:24).[3] Otherwise, for Paul, "the body of Christ" is not the same thing as the church. Actually, Paul never puts "the body of Christ" side by side with the church. Rather, whenever he refers to the church, he connects it with God: "the church of God" (1 Cor 1:2; 10:32; 11:22; 15:9; 2 Cor 1:1; Gal 1:13), not the "church of Christ."[4] Obviously, this lens of Paul's theology is very important because it is impossible to explore New Testament theology without Christ's faithfulness to God's kingdom.

Then, I came to realize that I needed to write a new book on Paul's overall theology. In *A Theological Introduction to Paul's Letters: Exploring a Threefold Theology of Paul*, I reinterpret three related genitive phrases—*dikaiosyne tou theou* ("the righteousness of God)," *pistis christou* ("the faith of Christ"), and *soma christou* ("the body of Christ")—as either subjective or attributive genitives.[5] The point is that God is righteous (God's righteousness), Christ is the one who is faithful (Christ's own faithfulness), and followers of Jesus are those who have to live like Christ ("You are a *Christic body*"). This reading of Paul's theology raises a serious ethical question about individual justification once and for all. Paul's primary concern is not how one can be saved, but how all, Jews and Gentiles, can stand in a right relationship with God. The snapshot of Paul's threefold theology is seen in a single verse, Rom 3:22—"God's righteousness through Christ's faithfulness for all who have faith." This threefold theology of Paul becomes a foundation for an alternative New Testament theology which involves God, the Messiah, and participants (followers of Jesus).

After wrestling with Pauline theology, I wrote *Biblical Interpretation: Theory, Process, and Criteria* to address biblical interpretation in general.[6] Here, I explore a unique strategy of biblical interpretation with a focus on three elements of interpretation—the reader, the text, and the reading lens. While celebrating the diversity of biblical interpretation, I conclude

3. Kim, "Reclaiming Christ's Body," 20–29.

4. Ibid., 24.

5. Kim, *Theological Introduction*.

6. Kim, *Biblical Interpretation*.

not all interpretations are valid, legitimate, or healthy because interpretation involves the complex process of what I call critical contextual biblical
interpretation. When we read the Bible, we should ask each time: *Why do
we read? How do we read? What do we read?* Since all text is contextual and
every reader brings to the text his or her own hermeneutical choices or
lenses, the text is more than an object to be uncovered; rather, it is a "dia-
logical" document that needs the interpreter's engagement, both critically
and contextually in ancient and contemporary contexts.

Then, in *A Transformative Reading of the Bible: Explorations of Holis-
tic Human Transformation*, I dealt with matters of human transformation
when we read the Bible.[7] On one end of the spectrum of biblical interpretation, the tendency is to emphasize individual salvation or a change of
heart that does not involve a communal or social transformation. On the
other end, the tendency is the opposite; what is emphasized here is a social
transformation without talking about a personal transformation. While the
former represents a traditional side of Christianity that seeks individual
salvation alone, the latter represents hosts of liberation hermeneutics such
as liberation theology, postcolonial, and feminist interpretations. These extremes need to be addressed, and we need to find a middle ground that in-
corporates both personal and public transformations. Obviously, this idea
of transformation in biblical studies is important to reformulating New
Testament theology, which is about a change in people and in communities.

In my most recent work, *Truth, Testimony, and Transformation: A
New Reading of the "I Am" Sayings of Jesus in the Fourth Gospel*, I challenge
the traditional reading of the "I am" sayings of Jesus.[8] Investigating various
contexts of the "I-am sayings" in Jewish and Hellenistic traditions, including the immediate context of the Johannine community, I argue that Jesus
in John's Gospel is thoroughly the Jewish Messiah (low Christology) and his
"I am" sayings should be understood as the works of God that Jesus does,
which are not his own. This way of reading the "I am" sayings of Jesus gives
us "a voice of inclusivism rather than exclusivism, solidarity rather than
marginalization, and liberation rather than oppression,"[9] because Jesus in
the Fourth Gospel asks us to engage in God's love for the world. This last
book is also critical to my exploration of New Testament theology because

---

7. Kim, *Transformative Reading*.

8. Kim, *Truth, Testimony, and Transformation*.

9 Ibid., ix.

the context and work of the historical Jesus in the Fourth Gospel is relevant to my purpose for this book.

All of the above works gradually led me to write this book on New Testament theology. In doing so, my take on New Testament theology is distinct. First, I emphasize the reader's deliberate decision-making when he or she is faced with interpretive options. That is, readers have to choose which view of faith can be followed. For example, whereas in the undisputed letters of Paul, faith means ongoing dynamic participation in Christ's death, in later epistles (Deutero-Pauline or Pastoral letters of which Paul's authorship is disputed), it has to do with "what to believe" (depository faith). Readers have to discern what is good and acceptable as they do theology today. Second, I reclaim Paul as a Jewish reformer who understands Jesus well and continues his work. In fact, Paul was fairly misrepresented in scholarly works. Some read him as the pioneer of Christian faith, especially in the matter of salvation based on "justification by faith," or as the founder of the church. Others see Paul as a betrayer of Jesus, who moves away from Jesus' teaching. But Paul correctly interprets Jesus with a focus on God's righteousness, which is interchangeable with God's rule in the Gospels. Paul's letters will help us understand who Jesus is. Third, the Fourth Gospel will also be very helpful to understanding the historical Jesus, as I mentioned before.

NEW TESTAMENT THEOLOGY IN A POSTMODERN WORLD

I situate New Testament theology within a larger religious discourse in human culture—in some sense of a postmodern world where some may say religion is an antique, while others may say all religions are essentially the same since all seek the ultimate truth in different ways.[10] Although we

10. Smith, *Why Religion Matters*, 23–41. For general definitions of religion, see http://www.studyreligion.org/what/index.html. Religion's relation to the world is understood as follows: a) religion and nature, b) religion and divinity, c) religion as ultimate concern, d) religion and the sacred, e) religion and meaning, f) religion and profound experience, g) religion as psychological, h) religion and the social, i) religion and power, and j) religion and science. The aspect of religion and nature emphasizes the difficulties of nature that are dealt with through religious resort. This mostly comes true to ancient primitive people and civilizations. Religion is needed because of natural disasters so to speak. While the aspect of religion and divinity emphasizes divine activities in the world, the aspect of religion and ultimate concerns has focus on ultimate questions such as where we are from or where we are going. While the aspect of religion and the sacred emphasizes the

live in a postmodern intellectual world, one thing that remains clear is our quest for ultimate questions such as *what is the meaning of life?* and *where do we go from here?* Even though our knowledge increases, there remains a "spiritual" area that we cannot adequately answer—the realm of *mythos*, which is the language of religion. Based on Karen Armstrong's discernment between *logos* and *mythos*, I say we need *mythos*.[11] For example, when an earthquake destroys innocent lives, the language of *logos* says the earthquake is but a natural disaster that can occur. It is the language of science, and we need to know this fact. But from the perspective of a victim's family, that explanation is not enough because there are different sorts of questions that we ask: Why did this happen to my family? Why was my beloved's life taken? Even though the earthquake is a natural phenomenon, its effects can be personal. So there is the need to comfort those who are affected so that they may persevere.

Oftentimes religion has not played a positive role as it has become a hotbed of conflict and hatred in places like Eastern Europe or the Middle East. But as we saw before, we need it because it helps us to live meaningfully in this world. In this regard, Edward Said observes, "Attacking the abuses of something is not the same thing as dismissing or entirely destroying that thing."[12]

---

experience of the sacred, separate from the everyday life, religion and meaning has focus on the role of religion in bestowing value or significance to human existence. While the aspect of religion and profound experience emphasizes special experiences of individuals with the divine, the aspect of religion as psychological deals with the psychological aspects of human lives. While the aspect of religion and the social emphasizes the role of religion in maintaining communities or society, the aspect of religion and power deals with tensions between those in power and those powerless. Lastly, the aspect of religion and science explains religion scientifically, using human biology and physiology. All of these aspects are not mutually exclusive, but there is a differing emphasis, for example on nature, divinity, ultimate concern, and so forth. The bottom line is religious studies can involve all or partial concepts of these because religion is a phenomenon of human quest for these various meaningful lives. This book uses this general approach to religion to which the Jesus movement (or Christianity) belongs.

11. Armstrong, *Case for God*, 304. She argues that logos cannot be messed up with mythos. Each has a role to play, and yet the two cannot be mixed. For example, catching a cold is a matter of physical thing and cannot be explained through faith or magic. This is the case for the fact that religion and science are different. But at other times faith (mythos language in religion) needs reason (logos language) because blind faith is dangerous in human lives.

12. Said, *Humanism and Democratic Criticism*, 13.

Therefore, our job is not to abandon religion altogether but to recover it in a good way, turning it into a powerhouse for all who need comfort, energy, insight, and empowerment. In fact, nobody can live without faith. Nobody can live a single day without having the faith that the earth is secure. We believe that the sun will rise tomorrow and that we will awake from our sleep in the morning. Faith is not a set of knowledge or teaching but a life blood that sustains every day and moment of our lives. Especially when we deal with difficult questions regarding human origin, existence, and life after death, we become religious or spiritual in some sense. In difficult moments of our lives, nihilism or a desultory outlook would not be a healthy option. Given human frailty and limitations, there is a great need to fill the gaps and lacunae in our lives.

Living in this postmodern world, we have to ask critical questions about Christian good news and Jesus in particular: Is Christian faith still viable in a postmodern world? Is the heart of Christian good news (gospel) viable in our time? How can we read the Bible or the New Testament in particular? Who is Jesus or is Jesus still relevant to our day? If so, how do we know? What is Jesus' view of God? What did he try to achieve in his life? What is his political view of the time? Did he think of himself as the Messiah? What brought him to death? What happened after his death? Was he resurrected or was he claimed as resurrected? What is the nature of resurrection talk in first-century Judaism in Palestine? All of these questions are enmeshed in matters of politics and religion. Otherwise, we cannot simply separate theology from politics. For example, Jesus' view of God involves both matters of theology and of politics since the Jewish God is distinguished from other deities in some respects. Of course, I do not intend to answer all of these questions in this book, but the point is that they are critical questions that we dare struggle to answer in a postmodern world where still many people seek the truth of God in the midst of facing a plethora of new issues in their lives.

It is my conviction that Jesus and early Christians must be understood in terms of their efforts to make a difference in a harsh world. Because of that, we can explore what they did, discerning what we can learn from them to relive the legacy of God's work for today. In doing so, I firmly believe that the Christian good news can contribute to the world at large. Doctrines do not save but God's good news does if there is the right participation from humans.

With the need of addressing postmodern sensibilities, this book has several audiences in mind. The first group is scholarly readers who are interested in New Testament theology, as this book does not follow the traditional dogmatic approach to the New Testament and its theology. This book highly values the reader's critical judgment about Jesus and the Jesus tradition. The other group is those who are skeptical about the New Testament or Christianity as a whole. To them this book presents a fresh new reading of the historical Jesus and the theological significance of his life which is still applicable to our lives today.

CHAPTER OUTLINES

Chapter 2 will have prefatory remarks for discussion of New Testament theology: Scripture, the Hebrew Bible, and the New Testament. Here, we will see what Scripture means in world religions and how New Testament writings are related to it. Then we also have to see what the Hebrew Bible (the Old Testament) is and how we should understand it in terms of New Testament theology. Then, more specifically we are concerned with the nature of the New Testament itself and its relation to the Hebrew Bible and New Testament theology.

Chapter 3 will explore Jesus' identity as a point of departure for/in New Testament theology. Jesus' identity is understood as what is knowable about him in terms of his unique personality distinguished from others, including his particular behavior or motives. With this definition, we will ask: What is Jesus' primary self-understanding? What brought him to certain behaviors or acts? How was he different from others? My aim here is a historical exploration of Jesus' identity, and I will zero in on his life conditions or struggles in Palestine, Galilee in particular. The most helpful identity information comes from Jesus' birth, upbringing, and adulthood.

Chapter 4 deals with the work of Jesus. There are three important theological phrases in the New Testament that can help us understand the work of Jesus, namely, "the good news of God" (*euangelion tou theou*), "the kingdom of God" (*basileia tou theou*), and "the faith of Christ" (*pistis christou*). The first two primarily appear in the Synoptic Gospels, and the last one in Paul's undisputed letters. "The good news of God" is what Jesus proclaims at all risks; it is about God and God's good news. Jesus' proclamation of good news is about God's rule against Rome's rule. "The faith of Christ" is understood as Christ's faith through which we get to see his works of

God's righteousness. Using these crucial phrases, we will explore the work of Jesus in the New Testament.

Chapter 5 deals with the death of Jesus. Putting the death of Jesus in a historical context, this chapter will argue that his death on the cross is a result of his proclamation of God's rule in the here and now. While the later epistles (Hebrews, Deutero-Pauline letters, 1 Peter) emphasize the meaning of Jesus' death with a focus on the forgiveness of sins or on a perfect sin offering, Paul's undisputed letters and the Gospels show quite a different view of Jesus' death, that being a result of his faith journey aimed at proclaiming the good news of God—a radical rule of God in an unjust world. For this purpose, texts of the New Testament will be examined.

Chapter 6 deals with the resurrection of Jesus. Examining the context and development of the resurrection idea in the Hebrew Bible and Second Temple Judaism, this chapter will clarify the meaning of the resurrection dominant during Jesus' time and throughout the Jesus movement. While resurrection narratives in the Gospels are conflicting with one another in detail, they can be read as a spiritual story that Jesus became "a life-giving spirit" that continues to be with his followers, rather than as a literal, bodily resurrection story. As a result, Jesus' followers continue to testify to the truth of God because of God's vindication of Jesus. The resurrection in the New Testament must include at least two dimensions of language: resurrection as a metaphor that emphasizes the importance of quality/value of life and God's victory/power against evil; and resurrection as a mysterious real presence of the spirit.

Chapter 7 will conclude the book by discussing some contemporary issues facing us, ranging from community to pluralism to ecology.

2

Prolegomena to New Testament Theology

BEFORE DISCUSSING NEW TESTAMENT theology, we need some prefatory understandings about the historical Jesus, Scripture, the Hebrew Bible, and the New Testament. So, we will briefly see how each of these has to do with New Testament theology. Oftentimes Jesus is not read in his context; therefore we need to put him in first-century Judaism in Palestine. Also, we need to correctly understand the nature of Scripture, which may contain both gems and detritus. So, discernment is necessary. Similarly, we need to have a correct understanding about the nature of the Hebrew Bible and the New Testament. With this kind of correct understandings we can explore an alternative approach to New Testament theology.

READING JESUS IN CONTEXT

Reading Jesus in context involves three dimensions of interpretation concerning the historical Jesus. First, we are reading Jesus the Galilean who lived in first-century Palestine and died on the cross. Second, we read the Jesus who has been claimed as the resurrected Messiah by his followers. Third, we also take the meaning of Jesus for our day.[1] For this purpose, we

1. As for the significance of Jesus, Graham Stanton is right when he says, "But all four Evangelists are concerned to set out both the story of Jesus of Nazareth and also what

raise the following questions: What can we say about him as he is understood from both historical and theological perspectives? What can we learn from Jesus and how can we continue the significance of his life and work for today, as we face tons of problems in all corners of the world, ranging from personal identity to climate change?

From the outset I will state a few things about how I approach the historical Jesus,[2] about whom New Testament authors generally write from their individual perspectives. First, Jesus must be understood within a broadly-defined religion through which he deals with various life issues in Galilee and elsewhere under the Roman Empire. In other words, neither did he come down from heaven to save lost souls or pay the price of sins nor did he come to found a new religion. Jesus lived his life as best as he could as a sincere and passionate Jew who proclaimed God's radical rule in the world. At the same time he dealt with all kinds of injustices that counteract God's rule. With this view, Jesus' work and death is understood as the result of what he was proclaiming about God's rule.

Second, accordingly, Jesus must be understood in Jewish prophetic tradition in which he challenges the religion of the day that serves only elites at the expense of the poor and the marginalized, as ancient prophets in Israel and Judah in the eight century BCE denounce rifts between the rich and the poor (Amos 5:24). All four gospels portray Jesus as a great prophet, albeit in different ways. In Matthew, Jesus is like Moses, but is more than or above him. In Mark, Jesus as a prophet goes through thorny roads of suffering because of God's good news that he proclaims (Mark 1:14–15). In Luke, Jesus is adamant about his prophetic ministry and ready to die (Luke 4:16–30). In John, Jesus came to testify to the truth of God (John 18:37), which is also the job of a prophet.

Third, the portrait of the historical Jesus is not equal to that of Jesus in the New Testament. Therefore the historical Jesus must be discerned in the New Testament. In general, later writings such as the so-called Deutero-Pauline letters (Colossians, Ephesians, and 2 Thessalonians), Pastoral letters (1–2 Timothy and Titus), and some of general epistles (1–2 Peters and

---

they took to be the significance of his action and teaching. Story and significance are intertwined." Stanton, *Gospels and Jesus*, 5.

2. By the historical Jesus, I mean a pre-Easter Jesus distinguished from a post-Easter Jesus. But I do not mean that the historical Jesus cannot be known through the New Testament. Unlike Rudolf Bultmann and others who discredit the gospels as mere products of evangelists, I find the canonical gospels helpful in understanding the Jesus of Nazareth. See Bultmann, *Theology of the New Testament*, 270–355.

Hebrews) tend to read Jesus from a very high Christology viewpoint in that Jesus is not differentiated from God. But the four Gospels and early letters of Paul (the so-called seven undisputed letters) contain a low Christology, which means that Jesus is the Jewish Messiah, not the same as God. Therefore, it is crucial to evaluate various materials about Jesus in the New Testament.[3] There are numerous areas in which scholars do not agree with one another concerning the identity, work, death, and resurrection of Jesus, all of which are touched on in this book.

WHAT IS SCRIPTURE?

Scripture simply means sacred writings in world religions to which the Bible also belongs. A broadly-defined concept of scripture contains both gems of resources for human transformation and hurdles that we have to overcome. At times certain scriptures give us narrow visions of human community, thus keeping us from seeing a more open, universal-value-driven humanity. An analogy of a water dam may be helpful. Water contained in a dam has the potential of becoming both positive, transformative energy if processed through an electric power plant, and negative, destructive energy if by a hole in the dam, the water floods an entire city. As for the positive effect of the scriptures, we may think of them as great assets of divine and human wisdom in world religions. Needless to say, the teachings of scriptures in Buddhism or in Judaism are very helpful to our moral spiritual lives today. Yet at the same time, some teachings or some texts in great religious traditions, including the Bible, may not always be helpful and in some cases would even be dangerous if we were to take them into practice today. For example, teachings about slavery or women in some New Testament texts are not followed by Christians today. If we do not properly interpret the Christian tradition and its scriptures, we would be irresponsible interpreters of the Bible, morally bankrupt and ethically insensitive to other fellow human beings. In fact, Jewish scriptures or Christian scriptures are not exclusive revelations that nullify all other scriptures of world religions. Judaism and Christianity are religions among others. The New Testament is not the exclusive reservoir of truths that makes void all other religious documents or experiences. The New Testament is a collection of various writings of early Christians who contextualized Jesus' teachings in their

3. For more about the historical Jesus studies, see Theissen and Merz, *Historical Jesus*.

lives. Otherwise, it is not the absolute revelation as if it gives us a single meaning about God or Jesus.

WHAT IS THE HEBREW BIBLE?

We also need to rethink the Hebrew Bible's nature and relation to the New Testament. The Hebrew Bible is called the Old Testament for many Christians and yet for Jews it is called the *Tanakh* (an acronym of Torah for the five books of Moses, Nevi'im for prophetic books, and Ketuvim for all other writings). The term "Bible" denotes "books," as the term is derived from *biblia* (books), the plural noun of the Greek *biblon* or *biblos* (a book). Therefore, it is simply a mistake to think of the Bible (the Hebrew Bible) as a single book.

The Hebrew Bible is a collection of many different genres edited and (re)written over the period of about one thousand years in different life-settings. There are different kinds of writings such as laws, psalms, prophetic writings, wisdom literature, court records, and apocalypse. Each of these genres is combined with a particular life-setting in which the story is told. For example, laws deal with a covenant community of Israel, starting with Abraham in Genesis 12, who is called by God, and promised to be the seed of all blessings. Psalms are about the personal or communal praise and lament about God in worship settings. Prophetic writings deal with the issue of justice in society. Wisdom literature covers ethics or wisdom by which individuals or communities have to abide. The bottom line is that the Hebrew Bible is a religious literature and yet it is a human medium that represents particular vantage points of people in particular times and places.[4]

Depending on the need of a community, views about God vary, often bringing in conflicting theology about God. In fact, there are four different views about God because of four different traditions (commonly known as J, E, D, P) involved in the composition of the Torah.[5] While J tradition

4. Trible, "Authority of the Bible," 2243–60. See also Ehrman, *Misquoting Jesus*, 11–15.

5. According to the documentary hypothesis theory, J source, probably developed during the dynasty of David in the tenth century BCE in Judah, emphasizes an anthropomorphic God who forms first human Adam, taking the dust out of the ground (*Adamah*) as in Genesis 2. This God smells sacrifice (Gen 8:21–22) and regrets the creation of humans. God comes down to earth (Gen 11:5–8) and sends angels. There seems no boundary between heaven and earth. This God becomes not only the God of Israel as they are promised and delivered from dangers but also the God of sovereignty for all. The Elohistic God source, originated in the Northern Kingdom in ninth century BCE,

emphasizes the anthropomorphic descriptions of God, E emphasizes the God of prophecy. While D emphasizes a system of reward and punishment, P emphasizes the holiness of God with ritual concerns. These traditions can complement our understanding about God; but at the same time, they do not always cohere with each other, in terms of perspectives or textual details. All of these traditions are the product of human religious experience; therefore, they cannot have the same perspectives or descriptions about God. Put differently, if the Bible had only one tradition or one voice, its authority would dwindle or be questionable because often that is the sign of dictatorship.

Because the Bible does not tell us all about God, the ultimate question is not what the Bible says but what we have to say about God in the Bible. In other words, we, as readers, have to exercise our judgment about what is written there. For example, if we find a merciless tribal God in the conquest narrative of Joshua, we do not need to justify such a God at all because the story is told by a particular people of Israel at the expense of others. Perhaps Josh 6:21 is notoriously unethical and asks for the reader's stance: "Then they devoted to destruction by the edge of the sword all in the city, both men and women, young and old, oxen, sheep, and donkeys." To my surprise, the congregation of a worship service that I attended said amen to this verse. What kind of God do they believe? What kind of ethics do they have? More surprisingly, we hear that the silver and gold, and the vessels of bronze and iron are saved from the destruction: "They burned down the city and everything in it; only the silver and gold . . . they put into the treasury of the house of the Lord" (Josh 6:24). Are living people and animals in Jericho not more valuable than the silver and gold?

---

emphasizes a God who speaks through dreams, prophets and angels. People have to fear God and behave with ethical conduct stipulated in the covenant. The Deuteronomic source, developed in the sixth century BCE when Judah was defeated, and during the Babylonian exile, emphasizes the God who punishes and restores his people only after people's repentance. A motif is a system of reward and punishment. There is no more unilateral love-relationship possible. Finally, the Priestly source, developed after the Babylonian exile (fifth century BCE), emphasizes the God of purity and holiness. Ritual is centered with the view of holy God. Order is important. Since the Priestly source is the lastly developed material/source in the composition of the Torah, priests took a control of the editing process. Not surprisingly, the Hebrew Bible begins with the Priestly material of the creation story in Genesis 1.

Myth and History

Therefore when we read the Hebrew Bible, we have to make a distinction between mythmaking and history. While myth has a role to play in the community in which it is told, it should not be confused with real history. Lots of miracles and miraculous stories about God can be read as myths that play a certain role in recreating a safe space under which the members of the community find comfort and strength for their survival. For example, the Exodus story (Exod 7–12) is read as a myth that gives meaning to the Israelites in that their freedom is because of God's grace. It is believed that the early stage of the exodus story begins with a few hundred Hebrew slaves at the Nile delta area (Ramses) who flee Egypt for their liberation at all risks. These slaves believe Yahweh would help them. They were on foot and could cross the marsh reeds or shallow lakes (not the Red Sea; the Hebrew word *yam suph* means "sea of reeds") without being struck down by the Egyptian chariots. The Egyptians gave up chasing them because they could not enter the lakes with chariots. Moreover, a few hundred slaves were inconsequential to the Egyptian economy. But to a group of these slaves, their escape was nothing short of a miracle. Reflecting on and remembering what just happened to them, these slaves firmly believe that this event is none other than a miracle, possible only through God's power and grace. The Lord (Yahweh) made it happen and their faith confirms it. This experience gives them words of confession and encouragement that God is the source of everything.

Actually, this miracle would not have been possible if they had not left the place of shackles in Egypt for a new home of freedom and justice. It was a miracle not because supernatural things happened but because what they thought was impossible came true in their eyes. They could have been captured and killed, but in fact they were saved. Hebrew slaves did not wait for angels to come to rescue them in prisons or their working places. If they had stayed in their place with fear and despair, they would not have been able to enjoy freedom. Scholars believe that as time goes by, this seemingly simple story of faith that calls for action for liberation has been embellished and expanded. But the whole point of the story is not about the graphic, majestic description of how fleeing Israelites crossed the sea by the miraculous act of God, but about people's courage, faith, action, dream, and hope for a free home risking death.

Other than that, the story is not to be taken literal in that non-Israelites are enemies of God, as Robert Warrior vigorously rejects the one-sided liberation story of Exodus:

> The liberationist picture of Yahweh is not complete. A delivered people is not a free people, nor is it a nation. People who have survived the nightmare of subjugation dream of escape. Once the victims have been delivered, they seek a new dream, a new goal, usually a place of safety away from the oppressors, a place that can be defended against future subjugation. Israel's new dream became the land of Canaan. . . . This land, Yahweh decided, belonged to these former slaves from Egypt and Yahweh planned on giving it to them—using the same power used against the enslaving Egyptians to defeat the indigenous inhabitants of Canaan. Yahweh the deliverer became Yahweh the conqueror.[6]

As we see here, the issue is not simply what the Bible or God says but what we have to discern is acceptable to follow. The Bible in general does not give us a single story or meaning. The Bible reflects multifarious communities in different times addressing very different issues and theologies.

WHAT IS THE NEW TESTAMENT? ✳

We also need to rethink the New Testament's nature and its relation to Jesus or New Testament theology. The New Testament can be understood diversely, as literature, interpretation, and theology.

The New Testament as Literature

First of all, the New Testament is a collection of early Christian writings, written in the 50s and mid-second century CE, comprised of various genres that contain stories about Jesus, God, and the world.[7] Most of the writings of the New Testament were written outside of Palestine, in major cities of the Roman Empire such as Antioch, Rome, and Ephesus. Paul stands out as an apostle devoted to spread the good news of God in the Gentile area, city after city. Since more Israelites lived in foreign lands than in Palestine in first century CE, we also see different levels of tension around the Jewish

---

6. Warrior, "Canaanites, Cowboys, and Indians," 279.

7. Borg, "A Chronological NT."

and Christian communities, as reflected in various writings of the New Testament, such as Galatians and Romans. Galatians shows that there is rivalry between Gentile Christians and Jewish Christians (or a better term is "Christian Jews" in the sense that their primary identity is Jewish). Paul's Letter to the Romans shows us that there was an issue of antinomianism by Gentile Christians who rejected the place of Israel and the validity of Law altogether. Paul corrects their view and affirms that God remains faithful to them (see esp. Rom 9–11).

Second, the chronological order in the New Testament is different from the canonical order, with Matthew's glorious gospel about Jesus in the first and Revelation's earnest expectation about Jesus' coming back in the last. Actually, according to critical scholarship, Mark is the earliest written Gospel among the four Gospels, and Paul's letters precede the Gospels. Paul's early letters written in the 50s tell us more about the vibrant character of early Christian lives, including the work of Jesus. Even though Paul did not directly write about Jesus, compared to the gospels, his letters are gems through which we may better understand Jesus' work. For example, Paul continues Jesus' work in terms of God's righteousness shown through Jesus' faithfulness (Rom 3:22). Therefore, in order to understand Jesus, we have to depend on Paul's experience too.

Third, the New Testament is the literature of early Christians who interpreted themselves in difficult times under the Roman Empire. Therefore, it contains the divergent conditions or issues with which they struggled in particular historical times under the Roman Empire. While some read the New Testament as literature with a focus on particular stories about Jesus and his salvific work, others primarily focus on Jesus' prophetic work. Through redaction-critical studies, we can identify a number of differences among the Gospels because each was written to address specific needs of specific communities.

The New Testament as Interpretation

The New Testament is not only a collection of various writings produced in different communities and in different times after Jesus, but the result of early Christians' interpretation of Jesus and God in their life context. The fundamental grounds on which New Testament writings stand are that Jesus is the Messiah who fulfills the Jewish scriptures.[8] Here the question

8. Ashton, "History and Theology," 5–6.

is, of course, how he fulfills them. In fact, the gospels do not agree on the significance of Jesus' work. Therefore, Jesus as a central figure of the New Testament must be examined in context, as we will see in later chapters. In the following, we will see how the New Testament as interpretation continues and discontinues the legacy of the Hebrew Bible. In general, what is continued with the New Testament includes positive aspects of God, who is the source of promise and righteousness for humanity. What is discontinued with the New Testament includes a merciless, tribal God image, the Jewish exclusive covenant, and the dominant view of the Messiah. What follows is the character of God with a focus on righteousness and promise.

God's Righteousness

God's righteousness can be best understood both in terms of his character and actions toward his people in the Hebrew Bible. God makes a covenant with Abraham and his descendants in Gen 15:1–21 (cf. 17:1–27). God's righteousness is well expressed with his covenantal faithfulness to Israel. Abraham did not do anything to deserve God's call. It is God's initiative, unilateral in nature. Even with all of the different images of God in Hebrew Scripture—such as father, husband, mother, king or judge—God is primarily characterized as the one who actually cares for his people in all circumstances, in good times or bad. God is always the ultimate reality that gives meaning to his people.

God's righteousness also can be understood as *hesed* which connotes various things: love (Mic 6:8; Hos 6:4, 6; 12:6), loyalty (Hos 4:1), and steadfast love (Hos 2:19; 6:6; 10:12). The whole picture of God's righteousness is made in view of "loyalty or faithfulness" and "steadfast love" through which both God and Israel are bound to each other. In this relationship, both are tied to be faithful. Likewise, God's people are to keep this relationship with others, based on love and faithfulness. To maintain this relationship with God and others, each has to show mercy and loving kindness. Accordingly, God's covenanted people are to live faithfully, to be worthy of God's call.

In the Hebrew Bible righteousness (*tsedaqa*) is synonymous with justice (*mishpat*), which means a range of interrelated things: justice, judgment, legal rights, vindication, deliverance, custom, and norm.[9] God is just because God cares for the poor and the marginalized. Amos is critical of those who do not care for the poor (Amos 2:6). Because God cares for his

9. Mafico, "Just, Justice," 3:1127–29. See also Mafico, *Yahweh's Emergence as "Judge."*

people, God's righteousness can also be understood as God's justice in an unjust world. God's righteousness means his unwavering protection and unfailing promise for his people (Ps 33:4–5; 36:5–6; 40:9–11).[10] The eighth century BCE prophets such as Micah or Amos make clear that God wants justice more than a burnt offering or noisy songs in the Temple. God wants his people to live in justice (distributive justice). God's justice also entails judgment when there is no justice in society. God can be a judge or plaintiff to defend the cause of the marginalized and the poor.[11]

Jesus basically testifies to this God of righteousness as we read in the Gospels and Paul's letters. In Mark 1:14–15, Jesus' first preaching is about the good news of God that has to do with God's rule (God rules! Not the emperor or any other authority). Similarly, Matthew follows Mark in this regard. Luke is more specific in ways that Jesus' first public preaching happens in the synagogue, telling his hometown people that his mission is to bring good news to the poor (Luke 4:16–30). This good news is about God's rule, which must be everyday reality in people's lives. God's rule is presently powerful in the community through the work of healing and restoration. Jesus in John's Gospel also makes clear that he testifies to the truth of God as he is confronted by Pilate. The truth for Jesus is to bring life and light to the world.

It is no question that Paul continues this tradition of Jesus in his gospel characterized with a threefold involvement of God, Christ, and Jesus' followers. God's righteousness (God initiates his love for people) is manifested through Christ's faith (Christ shows his faith) for all who have faith (Jesus-followers' faith in God or in Jesus).

---

10. In Amos 5:24, we may think of the distinction between righteousness and justice; righteousness is compared with the ever-flowing stream and justice with waters. The stream flows all the time like a stream without drying up or stopping. Righteousness has a comparatively quiet sound of flowing; it is like the quality of life, opening up to neighbors but not making noise but with gentleness. In addition, the stream is curved and varies in shape, but flows all the way without stopping, sometimes gradually making a new way, if needed, and at other times just passing over stumbling blocks. Justice is compared with waters analogous to the raging torrent. This image reveals visible power in which water rolls down with great energy. Justice is like this; it is more audible and visible. For more of a distinction between justice and righteousness, see Gossai, *Social Critique by Israel's Eighth-Century Prophets.*

11. See Kim, *Theological Introduction,* 38–62.

God's Promise

God's promise can be best understood against the backdrop of Gen 1–11 where humanity fails to serve God. People did not want to live according to the way of God. They sought a life of their own, becoming violent and destroying each other. Diversity, respect, and care were lost in the world; instead, what is prevalent is unilateralism and a power-seeking culture. The tower of Babel in Genesis 11 is a symbolic story that represents humans' resistance to God's will that people are to live with diversity and mutual care rather than with competition and control.[12] The world is in despair as time passes because of human greed, violence, and competition.

But in Genesis 12, we see a new beginning of promise for humanity by God who calls Abraham to leave for an unknown place. Abraham is a prototype of hopeless humanity which needs a new history of promise. He was neither chosen from the holy land but from Chaldea, Ur, nor was he picked out of a chosen race. He was a gentile of gentiles. He does not deserve a worthy call of God. God is the start of a new promise.

This is what Paul begins with in his gospel: "God chose what is foolish in the world to shame the wise; God chose what is weak in the world to shame the strong; God chose what is low and despised in the world, things that are not, to reduce to nothing things that are, so that no one might boast in the presence of God. He is the source of your life in Christ Jesus, who became for us wisdom from God, and righteousness and sanctification and redemption" (1 Cor 12:27–30). If the whole earth is God's, every part of the world is to be taken care of equally. If the hand suffers, the whole body suffers.

Because of God's initiative for a hopeful future, Paul acclaims that "Nothing can separate us from the love of God" (Rom 8:27). Our standing before God must be awesomely humble because nothing can explain our deservedness for the love of God. God breathes in us a new hope every day, sustaining us in any circumstances.

God of promise makes a covenant with Abraham that is the foundational belief that God loves his descendants. In good times or bad times, ancient prophets such as Isaiah, Jeremiah, Micah, and Amos spoke about God's covenant like a marriage relationship.

However, when there is a misunderstanding and malpractice of the Mosaic covenant, Jeremiah asks for a renewal of the heart, reminding the

---

12. Hiebert, "Tower of Babel," 29–58. See also Campbell, *Multitude of Blessings*, 27.

Israelites that God wants the heart, not mere observance of the law or any specious forms of religion. Thus Jeremiah speaks:

> The days are surely coming, says the Lord, when I will make a new covenant with the house of Israel and the house of Judah. It will not be like the covenant that I made with their ancestors when I took them by the hand to bring them out of the land of Egypt—a covenant that they broke, though I was their husband, says the Lord. But this is the covenant that I will make with the house of Israel after those days, says the Lord: I will put my law within them, and I will write it on their hearts; and I will be their God, and they shall be my people. No longer shall they teach one another, or say to each other, 'Know the Lord,' for they shall all know me, from the least of them to the greatest, says the Lord; for I will forgive their iniquity, and remember their sin no more. (Jer 31:31–34)

Otherwise, the idea of God's covenant or God's promise for a hopeful future cannot be used to justify the political ideological interests of the monarchical Israel. Using the covenant language, Solomon could enlist more labors for the building projects or for military campaign than otherwise. At other times, the Mosaic covenant becomes an ideological tool for excluding foreigners and political foes as we see in the post-exilic literature (Nehemiah or Ezra). Can the promise of God's covenant and of the new land allow the destruction of other people, the Canaanites? No way!

The New Testament as Theology

The New Testament is also a story about God, the Messiah, and the world that the early Christian communities retold in their life context. From the New Testament we know what God has done through Jesus or what God is concerned with in this world or what Jesus has done for God and the world. More than this, we also know how early Christian communities have lived for the good news of God because of Jesus. The New Testament is also a source of theology for contemporary readers/Christians who continue to do their part of theology in relation to God, the Messiah, and the world.

As a theological story of God, the Messiah, and the world, we must carefully reexamine NT texts, dismantling, redefining, or reconstructing methods and contents of New Testament theology. In terms of methods, doctrinal, deductive methods are deconstructed; instead, open-ended liberal approaches to religion or scriptures will be explored. For example, the identity and work of Jesus can be understood through his faith (*pistis christou*)—the Messiah's love of God and the world—that helped to disclose God's righteousness or God's kingdom in the world. What matters for our relation to Jesus is not our faith in Jesus but his faith that we have to imitate in our lives. Likewise, as we will see in later chapters, we have to deconstruct and reconstruct crucial theological phrases such as "the righteousness of God" (*dikaiosyne theou*) and "the kingdom of God" (*basileia tou theou*).

WHAT IS NEW TESTAMENT THEOLOGY?

Traditionally, New Testament theology has been read harmoniously, supporting particular church dogmatic theology such as the doctrine of "justification by faith." But the New Testament is not a harmonious document at all. Furthermore, some dogmatic theology is not well grounded in the New Testament. A typical case will be the doctrine of "justification by faith," which is not well rooted in early letters of Paul (the undisputed letters of Paul); such a thought is found in Deutero-Pauline and Pastoral letters. So our task is not to find a unified theology in the New Testament but to discern which theology or view of God or Jesus we should take in our understanding of New Testament theology.

As we see here, the tendency of New Testament theology is either promoting a conventional biblical theology characterized by the unified, doctrinal approach to the New Testament or abandoning New Testament theology altogether.[13] In the former, Jesus is read as the Son of God, fully human and fully divine, who reveals God in him and dies for the forgiveness of sinners. Jesus is the way to heaven and provides eternal life because of his vicarious death.[14] The critical question is twofold: Is this doctrinal reading of New Testament theology representative of the historical Jesus or of Jesus' early followers? The answer is a resounding *no* as we will see throughout the book. In many cases, New Testament theology or the New Testament itself became servant to doctrinal theology. In the latter, one group of scholars is merely interested in matters of history, whether from the historical Jesus or from the Evangelists. They dig up all kinds of material

13. See Morgan, "New Testament Theology," 472–80. See also Caird, *New Testament Theology*, 1–17; Via, *What is New Testament Theology?* 7–29.

14. Bernard Weiss and Heinrich Julius Holtzmann have a doctrinal focus of the New Testament. See Weiss, *Biblical Theology of the New Testament*; Holtzmann, *Lehrbuch neutestamentlichen Theologie*. See also Bella, *Challenges to New Testament Theology*.

to understand what happened to Jesus. Otherwise, there is no theological interest in studying the material in view of our lives or in terms of what God has done through Jesus.

But in fact, there are more presentations of New Testament theology beyond the two extremes above. William Wrede tries to establish an objective history of early Christian religion and theology. He suggests that we have to know from the New Testament "what was believed, thought, taught, hoped, required and striven for in the earliest period of Christianity; not what certain writings say about faith, doctrine, hope, etc."[15] In contrast, Rudolf Bultmann goes in another direction where he overtly engages New Testament texts in view of modern day concerns framed by existential philosophy.[16] Interestingly, Heikki Räissänen takes a moderate position by taking both of these scholars seriously. He argues that New Testament theology must include "the history of early Christian thought" and "critical, philosophical, ethical and/or theological 'reflection on the New Testament,' as well as on its influence on our history and its significance for contemporary life."[17] Räissänen's view of New Testament theology is distinguished from his predecessors such as Wrede and Bultmann, precisely because he emphasizes the New Testament's significance for contemporary life, which means that New Testament theology must address the global audience beyond Christian readers. In that sense New Testament theology is not captive to the church.

A. K. M. Adam has a view of New Testament theology that stands out since his interpretive framework is postmodern and makes explicit the postmodern reading through which one can make sense of the New Testament.[18] The goal is not to know the New Testament but to engage with it in contemporary life, with a very critical and self-critical stance of postmodern approach. Lastly, Frank Matera, standing on the opposite side of Adam, holds onto the unity of New Testament theology.[19]

---

15. Wrede, "Task and Methods," 84–85.

16. Bultmann, "Primitive Christian Kerygma," 15–53.

17. Räissänen, *Beyond New Testament Theology*, 8.

18. Adam, *Making Sense of New Testament Theology*, 111–39.

19. Matera, *New Testament Theology*.

AN ALTERNATIVE APPROACH TO NEW TESTAMENT THEOLOGY

This book's approach to New Testament theology is close to Räissänen in terms of a dialogue between "then and now" and to Adam in terms of the reader's "free" and yet critical role in postmodern reading. Yet my approach is different from them as I explore relationships among God, the Messiah, and the world in New Testament theology. In addition, my reading balances between text, the reader, and ethics of biblical interpretation. Below is my definition of New Testament theology.

> New Testament theology involves both what the New Testament says about God, the Messiah, and the world, and how the reader evaluates, engages, or interprets diverse yet divergent texts of the New Testament, including difficult, sexist, and oppressive texts. The reader's task is not merely to discern what is good and acceptable in the New Testament, but also to surface its limitations by examining early Christians' disparate positions about God, the Messiah, and the world. Consequently, New Testament theology is constructed by the reader who deals with both the divergent texts of the New Testament and the historical Jesus to whom they refer. By carefully sifting through the layers of New Testament witnesses while acknowledging unbridgeable gaps between them and the historical Jesus, the reader, in view of all aspects of life in the first century CE and today, has to explore relevant relationships among God, the Messiah, and the world.

First of all, New Testament theology involves more than what the New Testament says; it has to do with the readers' critical engagement with the New Testament including the historical Jesus when they explore the relationships among God, Jesus (the Messiah), and the world. This means that we have to engage the New Testament comprised of both early Christian religious experience (about God and Jesus) and Jesus tradition, and discern "what is good and acceptable and perfect" (Rom 12:2), as we continue to do theology in our times. But at the same time, we have to reject certain oppressive, sexist voices (texts) in the New Testament. The reason is that New Testament theology is not encoded in the New Testament, but can be explored and discerned through the reader's continual critical response to the New Testament including the historical Jesus. Here, the reader is a critical, contextual reader who critically examines his or her world today as well as the NT texts.

In this sense, the role of the reader in New Testament theology is not different from that of critical biblical theologians who interprets biblical texts in their various contexts and in view of contemporary life. Neither texts nor the reader dominates their meaning. Strictly speaking, all interpretation, historical or not, is contextual because the reader is in the process of all interpretation. Of course, my take on New Testament theology makes the reader more responsible for the process and criteria of New Testament theology because New Testament theology is not fixed once and for all or dominated by any person or institution.

Second, Jesus is not the only topic or goal in New Testament theology contra the traditional view that "Jesus was the starting point and goal of New Testament theology."[20] It would be impossible to talk about Jesus without talking about God because Jesus reveals God in his work. Jesus is the Son of God sent by God who does the works of God. Though we will see this point throughout the book, suffice it to say now that Jesus in the Synoptic Gospels, Johannine literature, and early letters of Paul appears as the Son of God—God's special agent as the anointed (Messiah or Christ), who is clearly distinguished from God. In the Synoptic Gospels, especially in Mark, Jesus warns that nobody but God is good (Mark 10:18). Even in the Fourth Gospel Jesus does not say that he does his work or that he is God.[21] Never once does he say that; rather, Jesus always says he does the works of God, not his own, and that he is sent by God. Even though he says that he and the Father are one (John 10:30), he does not mean he is God or the same as God (in the sense of equality between them) but talks about unity in terms of a working relationship. An analogy would be helpful. If I say to my family members that we are one, nobody would think that my family members are the same person. Simply, I mean that we, as family, love each other and work together. New Testament theology would be misleading if we do not look at God to whom Jesus points. Therefore, New Testament theology needs to articulate Jesus' working relationship with God. Jesus is a Jew devoted to Judaism, though he is very different from other Jewish

---

20. This quote is from Caird, *New Testament Theology*, 346. See also Witherington III, *Message of Jesus*, 43. Jesus is part of New Testament theology even when we talk about Paul's gospel, which involves three parties: God, the Messiah, and followers. I explored this three-party relationship in Paul's theology or gospel in my book, *A Theological Introduction to Paul's Letters*. I have also argued that even the Fourth Gospel does not say that Jesus is God; rather, Jesus embodies the Spirit or the Logos, which is God's. See *Truth, Testimony, and Transformation*.

21. Kim, *Truth, Testimony, and Transformation*.

teachers. Jesus' initial preaching was about God's good news and God's rule. For example, in Mark 1:14–15, Jesus began to proclaim God's good news (*euangelion tou theou*) and did not proclaim himself. The contents of God's good news have to do with God's rule (the kingdom of God) coming now. We have to investigate how Jesus' kingdom preaching subverts Caesar's kingdom.

Third, just as the body without the spirit is dead, New Testament theology without the historical Jesus is dead because the former is built on the work of the latter. No matter how many gaps exist between the historical Jesus and the New Testament, New Testament theology needs a solid understanding about the historical Jesus.[22] This view of mine is radically different from those who deny the historical Jesus' significance in New Testament theology. Rudolf Bultmann stands out as a person who vehemently argues that New Testament theology does not depend on the historical Jesus, but it suffices with the New Testament itself because the center of Christianity is a proclamation about Jesus (*kerygma*).[23] Part of the reason that Bultmann denies connections between the historical Jesus and the Christ of faith is that the former is simply inaccessible through the latter (Albert Schweitzer's view). But more importantly, he does not need the historical Jesus in his "existential" theology that requires only faith in Jesus. But while the historical Jesus is clearly different than portrayed in New Testament writings, we cannot ignore the historical Jesus in New Testament theology not only because what Jesus did is a reflection of what he thought important in matters of theology, but also because we can learn theological lessons from the study of the historical Jesus.[24] Therefore, to better understand the historical Jesus in New Testament theology, we need to see down-to-earth experiences of Jesus in first-century Palestinian Judaism. This means we will approach Jesus' identity from below with low Christology.

---

22. Tuckett, "Historical Jesus" 243–44.

23. Bultmann, "Primitive Christian Kerygma," 15–53. Before Bultmann, Martin Kähler already had such views that the historical Jesus is simply inaccessible; he says the "historic, biblical Christ" is "the real Christ" who is sufficient to Christian faith. See Kähler, *So-called Historical Jesus*, 43, 61.

24. Ernst Käsemann is the one who challenged R. Bultmann's view of New Testament theology and argues that New Testament theology needs the historical Jesus. The so-called "New Quest of the Historical Jesus" began with him, derived from his work, "Problem of the Historical Jesus," 15–47. Käsemann notes that "the question of the historical Jesus is, in its legitimate form, the question of the continuity of the Gospel within the discontinuity of the times and within the variation of the kerygma" (46).

SUMMARY

With the above definition/characteristics of New Testament theology, we redefine source, location, and subject of New Testament theology. First, as seen above, the source of New Testament theology includes both the New Testament and the historical Jesus. This requires us to carefully examine various writings in the New Testament and the historical Jesus to whom they refer.

Second, New Testament theology has its location in *this world* (*kosmos*), which means it begins not with special revelation from above but in the here and now when early Christians and followers of Jesus seek the meaning of life. This kind of anthropological approach casts its lot with a liberal understanding of religion that seeks the meaning of life in this world. All religions deal with human issues in one way or another.[25]

Third, in this alternative approach, the focus is not on doctrinal topics such as salvation or Christology, but on anthropological or political topics centered on the relations between God, the Messiah, and the world. These topics can be explored with the Jesus tradition under the Roman Empire.

With this new approach to New Testament theology, I hope that New Testament writings and the historical Jesus can make sense in dealing with contemporary issues ranging from personal identity to climate change. This new contribution to New Testament theology is possible through a renewed understanding of God, the Messiah and those who follow Jesus. God is righteous and demands justice in the world. Jesus as the Messiah showed his faith by his costly proclamation of God's rule (*basileia tou theou*) in the here and now. Christians are the followers of Jesus who are asked to imitate him in matters of life when they relate to this world.

25. See "Why Study Religion?" in American Academy of Religion website where various definitions of religion are found: http://www.studyreligion.org/why/.

3

The Identity of Jesus as a Point of Departure for New Testament Theology

BECAUSE NEW TESTAMENT THEOLOGY needs the historical Jesus, our first task is to explore his identity. Who was he as a historical figure? Jesus' identity is understood in the sense of who he was, including both his unique personality distinguished from others' and his behavior or motives.[1] With this definition, we will ask the following questions: Who did Jesus think he was? What motivated him to certain behaviors or actions? How was he different from others? How was Jesus understood by his followers after him?

---

1. This definition is different from Hans Frei, who understands Jesus' identity in terms of realistic, narrative presence in the Gospels and the Christian community. Like Frei, I also believe that the question of Jesus' identity certainly goes beyond historical knowledge about him because Jesus affects many followers and people after him. But I believe that Jesus' identity must begin with historical study about him. See Frei, *Identity of Jesus Christ*, 32.

My aim here is a historical exploration of Jesus' identity.[2] I will zero in on his life conditions or struggles in Palestine, Galilee in particular.[3]

However, sources for the identity of Jesus are very limited. We do not know his family background or what he did until the age of thirty (Luke 3:23). Surprisingly, Mark begins his Gospel with the baptism of Jesus in the Jordan. Perhaps it is because Mark judges that Jesus can be best understood through the last year of his life. But the reality is we have to depend on texts of the New Testament because there are no direct or earlier writings about Jesus except for Josephus's brief mentioning in the *Testimonium Flavianum* whose authenticity is, however, fairly disputed.[4] The question is how much can we depend on the New Testament as we reconstruct the identity of

2. My view of Jesus' identity is contrasted with that of a book, *Seeking the Identity of Jesus: A Pilgrimage*, edited by Beverly Gaventa and Richard Hays, where contributors theologically read Jesus' identity from their various hermeneutical lenses. In other words, there is no real interest in the historical Jesus' struggle or interest in the poor, as he is believed to experience poverty in Galilee.

3. Otherwise, I do not depend on psychological studies in my exploration of Jesus' identity. But I will touch on the psychological aspects of Jesus' identity insofar as they make sense to the historical exploration of Jesus' identity. Compare with John Miller's study on Jesus employing psychological theories. See Miller, *Jesus at Thirty*. Justin Meggitt rightly points out the importance of the broadly-defined psychological insights into the historical Jesus study; however, he warns against direct application of modern theories in psychology to historical Jesus studies because psychological studies are too contemporary to apply to first-century people. See Meggitt, "Psychology and the Historical Jesus, 16–26.

4. *Jewish Antiquities*, 18.3.3 §63. The full text of Josephus is as follows: "About this time there lived Jesus, a wise man, if indeed one ought to call him a man. For he was one who performed surprising deeds and was a teacher of such people as accept the truth gladly. He won over many Jews and many of the Greeks. He was the Messiah. And when, upon the accusation of the principal men among us, Pilate had condemned him to a cross, those who had first come to love him did not cease. He appeared to them spending a third day restored to life, for the prophets of God had foretold these things and a thousand other marvels about him. And the tribe of the Christians, so called after him, has still to this day not disappeared." Translation of Louis H. Feldman, *The Loeb Classical Library*. The authenticity of this passage is varied. But I believe this passage is spurious primarily because this text seems to support Christian faith about Jesus. We can hardly believe Josephus would have written "He was the Messiah" because he was a believing Jew under Romans. Furthermore, early Christian scholar Origen (185–254 CE) says Josephus did not believe Jesus as the Messiah. The current text is from early church historian Eusebius (260–340 CE). See Feldman, *Josephus and Modern Scholarship*. See also Josephus, "Testimonium Flavianum: Josephus' Reference to Jesus." http://www.earlychristianwritings.com/testimonium.html. For a full discussion about authenticity of this text, see Theissen and Merz, *Historical Jesus*, 64–74.

Jesus? Below are four views about the New Testament's relation to the identity of Jesus.

VIEW 1

The New Testament is enough for knowing who Jesus is. In this view, whatever is written about Jesus is read plainly, based on a literalistic approach to the text of scripture.[5] The gospels are read as "records" of the past about Jesus. For example, Jesus' birth story in Matthew or Luke is read merely as a story of the miraculous virgin birth by the Holy Spirit which does not involve a human father. Along with this, the emphasis is on sinless Jesus who makes the perfect sin offering. Likewise, in this view, the title Son of God is no more than God. Incarnation in John 1:14 ("the word became flesh") is also focused on Jesus' divinity rather than on Jesus' embodiment of the Logos. In this view, these critical questions about Jesus are hardly asked: Who did Jesus think he was? What did he do for most of his life before the age of thirty? What brought him to death?

VIEW 2

The New Testament is read as history informed by faith that includes high Christology and Jesus' vicarious death, among others. This view is held by moderate Christian scholars such as N. T. Wright, who acknowledges the historicity of the New Testament and yet subsumes it under the rubric of faith.[6] For example, Wright argues that Jesus is Israel's long-awaited Messiah who ends a long history of Jewish exile and return by dying for the sins of Israel and the world.[7] Jesus' vicarious death ushers in a new kingdom of God. Otherwise, Wright does not articulate the cause of Jesus' death in a historical context, not to mention the significance of Jesus' work in an imperial world dominated by Rome. Instead, he focuses on the evil behind the political or religious scenes.

---

5. This view is held by a majority of the so-called evangelical or conservative scholars and church. For example: Marshall, *Concise New Testament Theology*. See also Schreiner, *Magnifying God in Christ*.

6. N. T. Wright, *Meaning of Jesus*, 32–52.

7. Ibid., 51.

VIEW 3 *Liberal*

The New Testament, though insufficient for the study of Jesus' identity or inconsistent in the portrait of Jesus, still preserves trustable memories (oral traditions) about the historical Jesus. This view poses a duality of Jesus in the New Testament. On one hand, the New Testament's portrayal of Jesus is quite different from the historical Jesus because it is a result of developing traditions about Jesus.[8] When stories about Jesus are told and retold throughout the regions in the Roman Empire, the Jesus tradition is reshaped in that people choose what to tell in light of the significance of Jesus' work in their lives. On the other hand, there is a trustable source or information about Jesus in the Gospels and other texts in the New Testament, as is suggested by Robert McIver, who shows the credibility of oral traditions through the study of human memory in early Christian communities.[9] In fact, most Jesus research scholars attempt to construct the identity of Jesus with this cautious view of the New Testament.[10]

VIEW 4

The New Testament is unfit for the study of Jesus' identity; it is essentially a Christian theological story that reflects the view of Jesus' followers. This view reflects the so-called "no quest of Jesus," and many historians gave up pursuing the historical Jesus since Albert Schweitzer's monumental publication in 1906, *The Quest of the Historical Jesus*. Interestingly, Rudolf Bultmann protects the Christian faith by separating the New Testament from the historical Jesus. He argues that Christian faith is not based on the historical Jesus but on the Christ of faith proclaimed by early Christians.[11]

---

8. For general insights about these developing traditions about the Gospels, see introductory books on the New Testament such as: Robert Spivey et al., *Anatomy of the New Testament*; Ehrman, *New Testament*.

9. See McIver, *Jesus, Memory, and the Gospels*. See also Dunn, *Jesus Remembered*. But I do not agree to Dunn's view of the historical Jesus, who is said to be a preacher of the imminent kingdom of God with an emphasis on the judgment of God. See *Jesus Remembered*, 479–80. Later in this chapter, I will discuss this matter.

10. Belonging to this group are Geza Vermes, Marcus Borg, John D. Crossan, E. P. Sanders, J. P Meier, and James H. Charlesworth, all of whom are the so-called Jesus research scholars or simply "Third Quest." See James Charlesworth's brief introduction to the third quest: *Historical Jesus*, 8–12.

11. Bultmann, *Theology of the New Testament*, 270–355.

His existentialist interpretation of scriptures keeps him from basing the good news in the work of the historical Jesus.

Among all these views outlined above, View 3 is most relevant because we can cautiously use the New Testament for understanding the historical Jesus. With this view, we will explore the identity of Jesus by focusing on the birth, the upbringing, the baptism, and adulthood of Jesus both from the historical Jesus study and the New Testament. Otherwise, View 1 is very problematic because the New Testament is full of various forms of figurative speech that cannot be read in ordinary literal sense. For example, in John 6:51 when Jesus says "I am the living bread from heaven," he does not mean he is literally the bread, as some Jewish hearers take it. That is a real irony. The bread here is a metaphor that points to God's word. Jesus seems to say that he embodies the word of God. View 2 also, while plausible, is not pertinent to a critical scrutiny of Jesus' identity because history is understood through certain aspects of faith at the sacrifice of political aspects of Jesus' work. View 4 is also very problematic because the New Testament obviously contains good information about Jesus. Although written for theological purposes at different times in different places during 50–100 CE, texts of the New Testament still provide us with a solid lens through which we come closer to an understanding of the historical Jesus.

THE BIRTH OF JESUS

We do not know why Mark does not include Jesus' birth story in his gospel and begins with Jesus' adulthood at his baptism. In Mark, Jesus is called the son of Mary, not of Joseph (Mark 6:3). Moreover, Joseph never appears in Mark's narrative. Since in Jewish tradition children are referred to as a son or a daughter of the father, "the son of Mary" is very unusual.[12] Because of this, it may be highly plausible that Jesus has an unnamed father, involving an illegitimate birth. In contrast, Matthew and Luke include Jesus' birth story to tell their audiences that Jesus is the special Son of God born by the Holy Spirit.[13] The point of the message conveyed by these Evangelists

12. In John's Gospel also there is a possible indication that Jesus is born illegitimately. One of the critics of Jews responds to Jesus in their heated conversation with Jesus: "We were not born of fornication" (John 8:41), "as if to imply, as *you* were." See Tabor, "A Historical Look at the Birth of Jesus."

13. To portray Jesus as the Jewish Messiah who fulfills the scripture, both Matthew

is not the virgin or the miraculous birth itself but Jesus' special status as the Messiah or the Son of God.[14] Otherwise, the virgin birth story is part of a technique that legitimates the birth of prominent figures like heroes in Greco-Roman times.[15]

Interestingly, Matthew takes the time and effort to explain Mary's pregnancy. When there is a difficult thing or fact that must be communicated to the reader, the story tends to be longer than otherwise, as we see from the example of Jesus' baptism story in Matthew. From a historical critical perspective, to say the least, there must have been an unnamed father of Jesus whom Matthew does not tell us. In fact, Matthew seems to know about the illegitimate birth of Jesus when "mention of the four women is designed to lead Matthew's reader to expect another, final story of a woman who becomes a social misfit in some way."[16] As we see here, Matthew seems to associate Mary with these other women of questionable moral character—hence the illegitimacy of Jesus' birth.

However, no matter what happened to her, Mary's seemingly onerous burden of life with a sense of disgrace is eventually transformed into her joy and honor because God blesses her.[17] In the beginning of the story, Mary's shame is evidenced when Joseph hears news about her conception that does not have to do with him. Thus he tries to cut off the relationship with her in a private, quiet manner so that she will not be shamed publicly (Matt 1:19). However, an angel appears to Joseph in a dream and tells him that the baby will be born through the Holy Spirit and to accept and take her as she is (Matt 1:20). This is a story of Immanuel ("God-be-with-us"); God is with Mary and Joseph in difficult times.[18] More than that, God blesses them as

---

and Luke connect Jesus' birthplace with Bethlehem (Mic 5:1). As David is anointed in Bethlehem (1 Sam 16:1–13; see also Luke 2:4, 11), Jesus is born there as king of the Jews and as the Son of David.

14. *Almah* in the Hebrew text of Isa 7:14 means "a young woman of marriageable age." But the Septuagint (the Greek translation of the Hebrew Bible) translates it as *parthenos*, which means virgin. Supposedly, Matthew refers to the Septuagint when he quotes from Isaiah. For a traditional historical literary approach to the infancy narratives, see Brown, *Birth of the Messiah*.

15. For example, the birth accounts of Plato, Alexander the Great, Augustus and Pythagoras involve some kind of miraculous birth. See Cartlidge and Dungan, eds., *Documents for the Study of the Gospels*, 129–36.

16. See Schaberg, *Illegitimacy of Jesus*, 33.

17. See also Miller, "Illegitimacy of Jesus," 24–36.

18. Mary's transformation appears in her Song (Luke 1:46–55) which informs us about her radical theology about God. She magnifies the God of justice who takes upside

parents of Jesus, who is the sign of Immanuel as Jesus is born to save "his people from their sins" (Matt 1:21).

In sum, whereas Mark and John choose not to tell Jesus' birth story maybe because it is not important to their audiences or simply because it needs to be shunned, Matthew and Luke choose to tell the birth story and transform it into the story of God's grace for Mary.

THE UPBRINGING OF JESUS

The New Testament gives us almost no information about Jesus' youth or growing environment other than his trip to Jerusalem with his parents at the age of twelve (Luke 2:39–52). If Joseph died early, Jesus had to grow up with Mary, along with four younger brothers and at least two sisters (Mark 6:3).[19] If Jesus knew early enough about his illegitimate birth, this fact may have shaped his view of family or community because we humans are influenced by memorable life experiences. There is evidence that Jesus is looked down upon by his village people, as indicated in Mark 6:3: "Is not this the carpenter, the son of Mary and brother of James and Joses and Judas and Simon, and are not his sisters here with us?" Likewise, Jesus' relationship with his family seems rough (Mark 3:20–21, 31–35; 6:1–6a), which is an embarrassment to followers of Jesus (a criterion of embarrassment for establishing authenticity of Jesus' sayings or action).[20] Jesus refuses to speak to his mother and brothers when they look for him (Mark 3:31–35). Instead, he says to a crowd, "Who are my mother and my brothers?" (Mark 3:33; Matt 12:48). "Here are my mother and my brothers! Whoever does the will of God is my brother and sister and mother" (Mark 3:34–35). "Truly I tell you, there is no one who has left house or brothers or sisters or mother or father or children or fields, for my sake and for the sake of the good news" (Mark 10:29). Jesus is not welcomed at his hometown because of his prophetic teaching (Mark 6:4; Matt 13:57; Luke 4:24; John 4:44).

---

down the status quo of society, lifting up the lowly like herself or Jesus. "He has brought down the powerful from their thrones, and lifted up the lowly; he has filled the hungry with good things, and sent the rich away empty" (Luke 1:52–53). This Song hardly makes sense if we do not relate Mary's radical theology to her social location or particular life experience in Galilee.

19. Le Donne, *Historical Jesus*, 51.

20. This criterion is established in historical Jesus study. See Charlesworth, *Historical Jesus*, 20–22.

Jesus' Occupation

In Mark 6:3, Jesus is referred to as *tekton* (wood-craftsman, carpenter, or stone-worker): "Is not this the carpenter, the son of Mary . . .?" In contrast, in Matthew 13:55, Jesus is referred to as the carpenter's son: "Is not this the carpenter's son? Is not his mother called Mary . . .?" Most probably, Jesus could be a *tekton*, as Mark 6:3 says. But Matthew changes "Jesus as *tekton*" (Mark 6:3) to "Jesus as the son of the carpenter" (Matt 13:55) because Matthew finds it embarrassing to accept Jesus as *tekton*. The conclusion is Jesus was a *tekton*, who had to earn a living for his family. This occupation has to be understood in his social, political environment.

Jesus lives close to the Jewish synagogue as Luke 4:15 implies: "When he came to Nazareth, where he had been brought up, he went to the synagogue on the sabbath day, *as was his custom*." Jesus is a Galilean or Nazarene according to the Gospel stories (Mark 1:9; 6:1; Matt 13:54, 57; Luke 4:16, 23–24; John 1:45–56; 7:41–42). Luke tells us that Jesus' hometown is Nazareth in Galilee, a town of nobodies and insignificance from the eyes of Roman officials or Jerusalem authorities.[21] It is a small, outdated, devastated place. But Galilee is known for its resistance against Rome or the power base of elites in Jerusalem or local provinces, as shown through peasant uprisings for change.[22]

Therefore, it is not difficult to imagine Galilee's significance to Jesus' upbringing because it is a place of resistance against domination by Rome or Jerusalem.[23] In fact, Galilee, known for its devastation and poverty, is one of the most isolated regions in Judea;[24] there is great animosity and rivalry between Jerusalem and Galilee. Many peasants had strikes against the

---

21. Regarding the landscape of Galilee, see Shillington, *Jesus and Paul before Christianity*, 40–42. See also Freyne, *Jesus, a Jewish Galilean*, 24–25. Freyne believes that Jesus admires God's splendid creation displayed in Galilee through which water is supplied to the other parts of the country, devoting to the love of the land and natural resources.

22. Regarding resistance movement and literature in Galilee and Judea in general, see Horsley, *Jesus and Empire*, 35–54. For a big overview of the time of Jesus, see Hanson and Oakman, *Palestine in the Time of Jesus*. See also Oakman, *Political Aims of Jesus*.

23. For an overview of life in Galilee, see Horsley, *Archaeology, History, and Society in Galilee;* Hanson and Oakman, *Palestine in the Time of Jesus*. See also Crossan, *Birth of Christianity*, 209–35; *Excavating Jesus*, 136–223. See also Halvor Moxnes, "Identity in Jesus' Galilee," 390–416. Moxnes argues that "Viewed from the perspective of intersectionality the system of domination by Herod Antipas and the Galilean elite as reflected in the Gospels reveals multiple and interrelated forms of oppression" (408).

24. See Horsley, *Jesus and Empire*. See also Oakman, *Political Aims of Jesus*.

harsh Roman rule and Rome's puppet power—high priests and the wealthy elites.[25] In this political, economic environment, Jesus seems to have cognitive dissonance between God's rule (*basileia tou theou*) and Galilee where people suffer from political, religious anomalies. As a Galilean boy, Jesus must have seen personal and communal crises due to a lack of adequate religious and political leadership. Jesus may have wondered where God was in this chaotic world and what really went wrong. It is possible that Jesus went and saw the unspeakable splendor of buildings and lifestyles in Sepphoris, the capital of Herod Antipas's ruling territory, located just a few miles northwest of Nazareth, Jesus' hometown. Josephus confirms that Sepphoris is "the ornament of all Galilee" and "the strongest city in Galilee."[26] Along with heavily-armed Roman occupation, we can imagine very luxurious lifestyle of elites in this city whereas Nazareth is left poor.[27] Interestingly, there is no mention of Jesus' teaching at Sepphoris or Tiberias, "the two leading Galilean cities of his day."[28] Tiberias, same as the name of the Roman Emperor, is on the Sea of Galilee, the new capital to which Herod moved in 20 CE. Though we do not know whether Jesus ever taught there, the above data and historical context suggest Jesus' reluctance of teaching there. That is, perhaps that place is too difficult or dangerous for him or those cities are considered less important compared with other poor areas. In the gospel stories, Jesus rather focuses on "the peasants in the towns and villages (Luke 8:1; Mark 1:38): Nazareth, Capernaum, Cana, Bethsaida, Chorazin, and Nain."[29]

In sum, we can hardly ignore Jesus' life or upbringing in order to understand his teaching and action. No person starts his or her life at the age of thirty. Though we do not have direct access to Jesus' life or good records about his upbringing, we cannot stop seeking to understand his upbringing so that we may have a better picture about Jesus' identity.

25. See Horsley, *Jesus and Empire*, 35–54. For a big overview of the time of Jesus, see Hanson and Oakman, *Palestine in the Time of Jesus*. See also Oakman, *Political Aims of Jesus*.

26. Josephus, *Jewish Antiquities* xviii, 27.

27. Freyne, *Jesus, a Jewish Galilean*, 144. For the impact of Sepphoris and Tiberias on the Galilean economy, see Reed and Crossan, *Excavating Jesus*, 151–53, 204–6; Fredriksen, *Jesus of Nazareth, King of the Jews*, 182.

28. Stanton, *Gospels and Jesus*, 152.

29. Culpepper, "Contours of the Historical Jesus," 73.

THE BAPTISM AND ADULTHOOD OF JESUS

Now let us examine the baptism and adulthood of Jesus. The Markan baptism story tells us when, where, and how Jesus' baptism happened (Mark 1:9–11). Jesus' baptism is a simple fact that does not need to be explained; it happened in the Jordan by John the Baptizer. Unlike Matthew (3:13–17), Mark does not explain why Jesus needs to be baptized. It is a simple fact. Unlike Luke (3:21–22), Mark does not omit the baptizer's name and the Jordan. These differences can be explained through redaction criticism. Matthew uses Mark as a source but finds it an embarrassment that Jesus is baptized by John because John's baptism is about "repentance for the forgiveness of sins" (Mark 1:4). Furthermore, another issue for Matthew is why Jesus is baptized by John since he is superior to John. Because of this kind of embarrassment, Matthew edits Mark and explains the need of the baptism of Jesus. On the other hand, Luke's omission of John's name and the Jordan reflects the importance of his Gentile audiences, who are largely indifferent to those details. The conclusion is, since Mark is a source and written earlier than Matthew and Luke, and since Jesus' baptism is embarrassing to early Christians, the simple fact is Jesus was baptized by John in the Jordan.

Historians conjecture that Jesus goes to the desert in his twenties and meets John the Baptizer, who mentors and baptizes him.[30] John the Baptizer appears to be a very radical Jewish prophet (Luke 3:7–9; Matt 3:7–10), criticizing Herod's taking of the wife of his brother (Mark 6:14–24; Matt 14:3–12; Luke 3:19–20), and proclaiming the message about God's rule and asking for repentance in the here and now (Mark 1:14–15; Matt 4:23; Luke 4:43). His message is vitriolic: "You brood of vipers! . . . Bear fruits worthy of repentance. . . . God is able from these stones to raise up children to Abraham. Even now the ax is lying at the root of the trees; every tree, therefore, that does not bear good fruit is cut down and thrown into the fire" (Luke 3:7–9).

There are some clues about John's social location, principal message, and his role in Jesus' life. First, John "was clothed with camel's hair, with a leather belt around his waist, and he ate locusts and wild honey" (Mark 1:6; also Matt 3:4). This peculiar life style in the wilderness is related to Jewish

---

30. Luke 3:1–2 situates John the Baptizer's ministry and Jesus' baptism in the fifteenth year of the reign of Emperor Tiberius, which means 29 CE.

prophets who do their prophetic works through symbolic acts.[31] Moses and Joshua take off their shoes while standing on the holy ground (Exod 3:5; Josh 5:15). Ezekiel symbolizes his prophetic work using his body: for example, his symbolic siege of Jerusalem (Ezek 4) and his eating of the scroll (Ezek 2:8–3:6). As Ezekiel utters a judgment for Jerusalem and the need for repentance, John delivers a similar message of repentance and judgment for Jews if they fail to embody God's rule right now (Mark 1:14–15; Luke 3:7–9; Matt 3:7–10). Second, John's preaching in the wilderness and baptizing at the Jordan must tell us about the centrality of his message for the Israelites. The wilderness represents the long journey of Israelites after the exodus because they did not follow God's will (Num 14:33–34; 32:13). John's choice of wilderness emphasizes the importance of repentance and renewal for people (Mark 1:1–6; Matt 3:1–6; Luke 3:2–14). John proclaims once again renewal of Israel at the Jordan—the historical river crossed by Joshua and Israelites on their way to new hopes directed by God (Josh 3:1–4:24).

Given John's peculiar social location and his message, it is not difficult to imagine how much Jesus would be influenced by him. After John was arrested, Jesus departs for his own ministry, proclaiming a similar message to John's: "The time is fulfilled, and the kingdom of God has come near; repent, and believe in the good news" (Mark 1:15). Jesus' proclamation of

---

31. Prophetic gestures (symbolic acts) are amply found in Jeremiah. For example, the prophet remains unmarried due to impending disaster (Jer 16:1–9). This is similar to Ezekiel not mourning his wife in the context of the city's overwhelming destruction (Ezek 24:15–27). This also recalls Hosea's symbolic marriage (Hos 1–3). Another symbolic act was the purchase of a jug (Jer 19) which he publicly smashes to symbolize how Yahweh will break his people. Another is the wearing of an animal's yoke on his neck (Jer 27—28) as a message to the kings of Moab, Edom, Ammon, Tyre, and Sidon who had formed a coalition with Zedekiah against Nebuchadnezzar of Babylon. The message is they will all be servants of the Babylonian king, so they must bring their necks under his yoke and serve him (27:12) in order to survive. This leads to opposition by the prophet Hananiah who breaks the yoke proclaiming that Yahweh will break the yoke of Babylon within two years (28:11). This recalls the encounter between Micaiah ben Imlah and Zedekiah son of Chenaanah who made iron horns to symbolize the destruction of the Syrians in 1 Kgs 22:11. Jeremiah ends as the true prophet whose word becomes true (Jer 23:18, 22). Another symbolic act is Jeremiah's purchase of a field in his hometown of Anathoth to symbolize that houses and fields will again be bought after Jerusalem has been punished for its sins (32:15, 42–44). Other symbolic acts include the purchase and hiding of a linen cloth (13:1–11) and burying stones in Egypt (43:8–13). The prophet also interprets ordinary events as Samuel does in 1 Sam 15:27–28 when Saul tears his garment (loss of his kingdom to David). Included here is the act of the potter making a clay pot, destroying the spoiled pot, and starting over again (Jer 18:1–12). Similarly a scroll on which Jeremiah's words are written is destroyed (ch. 36).

salvific

"time fulfilling" in Mark 1:15 is about God's time (*kairos*), which has come now and will continue. Now is the time. So God's salvific activity has already happened, and will continue to come. But God's radical rule does not come into reality by force. It must come through a change of mind and heart in the here and now, and also involve personal and political lives. If God's rule is not visible in the world here and now, what is it for? If Jesus' focal point of his message is God's rule "here and now," he is not a typical apocalyptic prophet or a fear-driven religionist who announces an imminent judgment of God. Rather, Jesus advocates a love-driven, practical religion that can make a difference in the world. Announcement of judgment can be understood as a form of ethical challenge to people so that they may change their hearts to seek God's way.[32] Thus, I am convinced that the apocalyptic reading of John and Jesus is greatly misleading. Actually, if people change their minds and hearts, the future is already here and now.[33] If we read God's rule and time in this way, John and Jesus are unlikely to be doomsday preachers focusing on future judgment, feeding a fear-driven religion into people's minds; they are prophets of real time issues, seeking God's rule into people's lives here and now.

THE TITLES OF JESUS

In exploring Jesus' identity, the question "what did Jesus think he was?" will be answered by studying the titles of Jesus in the New Testament: the Son of God, the Son of Man, the Messiah (Christ), and the King of Jews, to name a few. Obviously, all of these titles in the New Testament are very christological and portray Jesus according to their wishes. However, these titles have origin with the historical Jesus in ways that no title can be made out of thin air. Some titles such as the Son of Man or the Son of God may have been used by the historical Jesus although his use may be different from his followers.' Other titles such as the Messiah and the King of Jews are given more likely by his followers.

32. Borg, *Meaning of Jesus*, 53–76. See also Claus Westermann, who surveys forms of prophetic judgment throughout the Hebrew Bible. Westermann, *Basic Forms of Prophetic Speech*, 129–94.

33. Like John D. Crossan, I am convinced that Jesus' proclamation of God's rule is focused on the *here and now*; but I do not agree to his idea that Jesus' proclamation is contrasted with John the Baptizer's proclamation of the future kingdom of God. See Crossan, *Jesus: A Revolutionary Biography*, 48, 56; "Message of Jesus," 33–43.

The Son of God

From the outset, the Son of God in the Gospels or in the undisputed letters of Paul is not a divine title, but a metaphor that points to Jesus working for God with Jesus' special relationship with him.[34] Moreover, the New Testament as a whole does not confirm the doctrine of Trinity, the "three-in-one" God (God, the Son, and the Spirit). Sometimes 1 John 5:7–8 is read to support the Trinity by adding additional texts "in heaven, the Father, the Word, and the Holy Ghost; and these three are one. And there are three that bear witness in earth," which are found in the King James Bible.[35] But this addition does not appear in early Greek manuscripts but only in late manuscripts from fourteenth to sixteenth century.[36] At other times, the baptismal formula in Matt 28:19 ("baptizing them in the name of the Father and of the Son and of the Holy Spirit") has been read to support the Trinity; but this formula is not about the Trinity, but about God's work carried out through Jesus and the Holy Spirit. Otherwise, there is no clear-cut language of the three-in-one Godhead.

Rather, the Son of God can be better understood through Jewish tradition and in comparison with the Roman imperial ideology. In the Hebrew Bible, the "Son of God" refers to Israel (Exod 4:22; Hos 11:1; Jer 31:20), to the Israelites (Hos 2:1; Isa 1:2; Jer 3:19), or to the leaders of the people such as kings, princes, and judges (Isa 9:5; Ps 2:7; 89:27; 110:3). The Son of God is not divine but a human agent of God (king, prophet, or particular individuals) or refers to Israel in a collective sense. In this Jewish context, even if Jesus may have thought of himself as the Son of God, it does not mean that he is divine but rather a special agent of God (like a prophet). In first-century Judaism, the Son of God is not necessarily a divine title. For example, in John's Gospel Jesus appears to be God's agent, the special son of God who does the works of God (John 5:36; 6:28; 9:4; 10:25, 37–38; 14:11–12; 15:24). That is, Jesus as the Son of God embodies the Logos of God.

Also, the Son of God needs to be read against the imperial context where Caesar is claimed as the son of God (*divi filius*). Caesar dominates God's creation and does not do justice to all peoples; he is glorified at the

---

34. Charlesworth shows that in first-century Judaism, the term "son" refers to an ideal figure or redeemer. For example: in 1 Enoch 105:2; T. Levi 4:2; Wisdom 2:18; 4 Ezra 7:28; 13:37, 52. See Charlesworth, *Jesus within Judaism*, 149–151.

35. See Lightfoot, *How We Got the Bible*, 100–101.

36. Ibid.

expense of the poor and the marginalized. In this Roman imperial context, the Son of God is a political title that challenges this very unjust system. Jesus is adopted as the Son of God to fight other sons of God in the Roman Empire because they seek refuge in wealth and power without doing justice for all.[37]

The Son of God in the Gospels

In Mark, Jesus is adopted as the Son of God at his baptism: "And a voice came from heaven, 'You are my Son, the Beloved; with you I am well pleased'" (Mark 1:11). Like Jewish prophets called by God, Jesus is called, baptized, and declared as God's special agent, the Son of God. As the Son of God, Jesus walks a long, difficult path of suffering and risks his life proclaiming the good news about God's rule (1:14) until he dies on the cross. On the way to Jerusalem, a place of power and privilege, Jesus shows feelings of hesitation or anguish. The Son of God is "distressed and agitated" (14:33) and laments injustices done onto him: "My God, My God, why have you forsaken me?" (Mark 15:34; also Matt 27:36). All this shows bare facts about Jesus' humanity and the cost of sonship.

A Roman centurion's declaration about Jesus as the Son of God (Mark 15:39) seems to imply that Jesus as the Son of God is very different from other sons of God (Augustus or Tiberius) in the Roman Empire. Whereas Jesus risks his life for the powerless, emperors secure their royal seats at the expense of the powerless. Perhaps a Roman centurion recognizes a different kind of divine sonship with Jesus because of his other-centered life and sacrifice. Jesus as the divine son "came not to be served but to serve, and to give his life a ransom for many" (Mark 10:45). Here, "to give his life a ransom for many" must be understood as the cost of Jesus' proclamation about God's rule. So, it is not surprising that Mark begins his Gospel with "the good news of Jesus, the Son of God" (1:1), which means the good news that Jesus proclaims about God or God's rule.

In Matthew, since Matthew uses Mark as a source, the overall meaning of the Son of God is similar to Mark's, although Matthew's detailed characterization of the Son of God differs from Mark's. Jesus is adopted as the beloved Son of God at his baptism (Matt 3:17; 17:5). Jesus is chosen by God as his servant: "Here is my servant, whom I have chosen, my beloved, with whom my soul is well pleased. I will put my Spirit upon him, and he

37. See Peppard, *Son of God in the Roman World*, 49–85.

will proclaim justice to the Gentiles" (Matt 12:18). This adoption requires Jesus to be tested in the wilderness, and so is Jesus tested and qualified for God's work. Then, the Son of God does the work of God (Matt 8:29; 14:33) at all risks (Matt 26:33; 27:40, 43). Jesus' work as the Son of God is confirmed by a centurion who sees the difference between Caesar and Jesus (Matt 27:54); that is, the former is for his own power whereas the latter is for saving others.

In Luke also, the basic view of the Son of God is similar to Mark's since Luke uses Mark as a source for his Gospel. Jesus is called the Son of God by the power of the Holy Spirit (Luke 1:35) and is adopted as the beloved Son of God at his baptism (Luke 3:22).[38] Note here again the adoption language in that Jesus is anointed by the power of the Holy Spirit. He is also reaffirmed as the Son of God on the mountain (9:35). The Son of God is tested but wins the test (4:1–13) and does the works of God (4:41) at all risks (22:70). In particular, Jesus appears as a Jewish prophet and he is adamant about his prophetic mission. In Luke 4:16–30, Jesus preaches at the synagogue in his hometown and is almost killed because of his radical preaching about God's special love for the Gentiles. He says, "No prophet is accepted in the prophet's hometown" (Luke 4:24). He is not agitated before the impending danger that comes his way. He even prays, "Father, forgive them; for they do not know what they are doing" (Luke 23:34), and dies as a Jewish martyr for doing the works of God.

Even in John's Gospel, the Son of God is not a divine title, contrary to the popular view of high Christology.[39] Jesus defends himself against the charge of blasphemy in John 10:35–36: "If those to whom *the word of God*[40] came were called 'gods'—and the scripture cannot be annulled—can you

38. Interestingly, adoption language also appears in the Hebrew Bible with regard to David (the greatest King of Israel) who is identified as the Adopted Son of God (2 Sam 7, 1 Chr 17, Pss 89, 132); and the NT identifies Jesus as a Davidic descendent in Matthew's Gospel.

39. "The Son of God" appears in John 1:34, 49; 3:18; 5:25; 11:4, 27; 19:7; 20:31.

40. "The word of God" (*logos tou theou*) in 10:35 is God's word that Jesus embodies and delivers to his disciples or communities in his farewell speech (John 17:6–7, 14). "I have made *your name* known to those whom you gave me from the world. They were yours, and you gave me to them, and they have kept *your word*" (John 17:6). Jesus' emphasis of God's word continues: "I have given them *your word*, and the world has hated them because they do not belong to the world, just as I do not belong to the world. I am not asking you to take them out of the world, but I ask you to protect them from the evil one. . . . Sanctify them in the truth; your word is truth. As you have sent me into the world, so I have sent them into the world" (John 17:14–18).

say that the one whom the Father has sanctified and sent into the world is blaspheming because I said, 'I am God's Son'?" While accepting the title Son of God, Jesus does not agree to the charge of blasphemy because he does the works of God as God's servant, as he quotes from Ps 82:6 ("I say, 'You are gods, children of the Most High, all of you").[41] As opposed to the usual reading, even John 10:30 ("The father and I are one") does not mean that Jesus is the same as God; rather, Jesus talks about unity in terms of his working relationship with God. Jesus says they are one not because they are the same but because he does the works of God. Otherwise, Jesus makes clear that God the father is greater than he (John 14:28). In the Gospel narrative, there is no mention or hint that Jesus claims his equality with God. Even the idea of "begotten" is not found in John 1:14 and 18. The Greek adjective *monogenes* simply means "only" or "unique," implying Jesus' unique work of God. The Son of God in John is sent by God (John 4:34; 5:37–38; 6:28–29) and thoroughly does the works of God, not his own (John 5:36; 6:28; 9:4; 10:25, 37–38; 14:11–12; 15:24). "If I am not doing the works of my Father, then do not believe me. But if I do them, even though you do not believe me, believe the works, so that you may know and understand that the Father is in me and I am in the Father" (John 10:37–38).

The Son of God in the Undisputed Letters of Paul[42]

In Romans, Jesus is "declared to be Son of God with power according to the spirit of holiness by resurrection from the dead" (Rom 1:4). The language of declaration must be important in Paul's theology. That is, Jesus is not born as the Son of God, but declared to be Son of God because of his work for God; this declaration is done with the power of the Holy Spirit by resurrecting Jesus from the dead. Paul's language of declaration here is similar to Jesus' adoption at baptism in the Synoptic Gospels. Paul is specific as to why Jesus deserves such a title of the Son of God and summarizes his gospel in Rom 3:22: "God's righteousness through Jesus Christ's faith for all who have faith." This single verse expresses the gist of Paul's gospel (good

41. Additionally and more to the point, the Davidic king in 2 Sam 7 and 1 Chr 17 is the "adopted son of God." Similar references are also found in Ps 89 and 132. In other words, the Davidic king has a close, special, and familial relationship with God. He is not God. In the same vein, in Jewish context when Jesus is called the Son of God, it does not mean he is divine.

42. The undisputed letters of Paul, written in a period of 50–60s, predate all the Gospels and contain the vivid early Christian activities.

news) or theology. That is, God's righteousness (God's love and justice) is revealed through Jesus Christ's faith, and it is now available for all who participate in Jesus' faith. In Gal 2:16 also, Paul emphasizes the importance of Christ's faith that is crucial to the righteous life of his followers (Christians) before God. He says that a person is justified not by the works of the law but through "the faith of Jesus Christ" (*pistis christou*), which I interpret as Christ's faith (the subjective genitive).[43] Paul says a person can stand right with God by participating in Christ's faith that boldly embodies God's righteousness at all risks. Paul emphasizes the cost of Christ's faith, which challenges all sorts of abusive powers including political authorities. Because of this, Jesus' followers have to die like Jesus: "I have been crucified with Christ" (Gal 2:19). Furthermore, Paul decides to *live in* Jesus' faith: "It is no longer I who live, but it is Christ who lives in me. And the life I now live in the flesh I live *in the faith of the Son of God*, who loved me and gave himself for me" (Gal 2:20). In the end, because of Jesus' faithfulness (Rom 3:21–26; Gal 2:16–20), God's righteousness shines in the world so that the most vulnerable are called and gathered into the house of God (1 Cor 1:26–30).

After Paul

In post-Pauline churches there is no clear distinction between God and Jesus Christ, who is "the image of the invisible God" (Col 1:15) and "the reflection of God's glory" (Heb 1:3). Likewise, "For in him all things in heaven and on earth were created, things visible and invisible, whether thrones or dominions or rulers or powers—all things have been created through him and for him" (Col 1:16). He is preexistent: "He himself is before all things, and in him all things hold together" (Col 1:17). It is certainly plausible that here, high Christology serves to defend the community's faith against external threats: "Elemental spirits of the universe" (Col 2:8), angel worship (Col 2:18), obeisance to the elemental spirits or "principalities and powers" (Col 2:15). But at the same time, this high Christology contributes to a rigidly structured community with Jesus as the head of the church

---

43. Paul does not deny the validity of the Law in Galatians or in Romans. His point is that the law should be informed by faith and grace. God's promise or grace comes first in matters of soteriology; then faith comes (in God). No laws will precede God's promise of love and faith rooted in God's grace. That is why the issue of circumcision is not an essential mandate to the Gentile Christians in Galatia or elsewhere.

(Col 1:18). The church becomes Christ's. Not surprisingly, "the body of Christ" is used as a metaphor of an organism (Eph 4:12; 5:30; Col 3:15). Likewise, stringent gender relations are exacted in the community; women cannot teach in the church (Col 3:18—4:1; Eph 5:22—6:9; 1 Tim 2:10–15; 5:1—6:2; 2 Tim 2:20–22). This shift in post-Pauline churches is contrasted with Paul's teaching that the church is egalitarian and it is always referred to as God's church (1 Cor 1:2; 10:32; 11:22; 14:4; 15:9; 2 Cor 1:1; Gal 1:13). There is no hierarchy in church: "You are the body of Christ" (1 Cor 12:27); all members constitute Christ's body.

The Messiah (Christ)

The Messiah or Christ means "the anointed one" (*mashiah* in Hebrew and *christos* in Greek) and appears in a variety of contexts in the Hebrew Bible: priests (Lev 4:3, 2 Sam 1:14), prophets (1 Kgs 19:16; Isa 61:1; Ps 105:15), king (Ps 2), and Israel as a whole (Exod 4:21; Ps 2:7; Hab 3:13; Hos 11:1). Interestingly, Cyrus the King of Persia is also called the Messiah because he allows Jews in Babylonian captivity to return to Jerusalem (Isa 45:1). Overall, the role of the anointed one in the Hebrew Bible is public work done by the office of king, prophet or priest. But as time goes by, we see different images or models of the Messiah in the first century CE: the mighty warrior messiah (Hag 1–2; Zech 3:8; 6:12), the divine figure messiah (Dan 7:13–14; 8:16–18; 1 Enoch 46:1; 48:10; 52:4; Mark 14:62); "the messiahs of Aaron and Israel"[44]; the crucified Messiah in Paul's letters and the Gospels.[45]

It is very unlikely that Jesus thought of himself as the Messiah for the following reasons. First of all, if he knew about the typical figures of the Jewish Messiah, he knew that he was not close to being as powerful political leader as King David. His teaching and actions are different from revolutionaries or an armed resistance group such as the Zealots.[46] Though his

---

44. 1QS 9:10–11.

45. For an overview of pre-Christian Jewish messianism, see Collins, "Pre-Christian Jewish Messianism," 1–20.

46. Often Jesus is claimed as a revolutionary who endorses the use of weapons, and for such a claim Luke 22:38 is used: "They said, 'Lord, look, here are two swords.' He replied, 'It is enough.'" But in a close reading of Jesus' message throughout the Gospel and literary context of chapter 22, this verse is hardly to be supporting evidence for armed resistance. In v. 36, Jesus tells his disciples to take a purse, a bag, and buy a sword if they don't have, and all of these items are not for battle but for preparation for harsh times. Otherwise, Jesus does not mean that "two swords" are not enough for battle. Rather,

teaching involves personal and political changes (Mark 1:14–15), there is no hint in the Gospels that his teaching will be accomplished by violence. Second, Jesus prefers to call himself the son of man, as we will see later. Third, Jesus is not a sectarian leader like the one in Qumran community. The bottom line is that Jesus is not close to being like any type of Messiah in this time. Nonetheless, the New Testament claims that Jesus is the Messiah (Christ)—the Messiah crucified, which is a new idea that history has never seen. Indeed, for Jews it is unthinkable for the Messiah to be hung on the cross (Deut 21:22–23). However, the Evangelists and Paul argue that the crucified Messiah is evidence of God's power, God's victory, and God's wisdom. According to the Gospel stories and their logic, Jesus the Messiah shows God's power by challenging evil and unjust powers against God's rule. As a result, he is crucified. But God resurrects him because of his faithful work. God vindicates him; the crucified Messiah did not fail. Likewise, Paul also has a similar view with the Gospels. According to Paul, the cross is God's power and wisdom even though Christ crucified is "a stumbling block to Jews and foolishness to Gentiles" (1 Cor 1:23). The reason is through Christ's faith and life, God's power is manifested in the world in the midst of abusive powers and self-seeking worldly wisdom (1 Cor 1:24–25). Jesus' death is a result of his faithful life. Otherwise, the death of Jesus is not the precondition for the Messiah.

The Son of Man

The title Son of Man in the New Testament appears in three different ways: 1) Jesus' self-referral in the Gospels (Mark 9:31; 10:33–34), 2) a prophet representative such as Ezekiel who receives God's call and works for God (Ezek 2:3–4; 4:1–7; 17:2),[47] 3) a cosmic figure found in Daniel 7:14 and in *The Similitudes of Enoch* (1 Enoch 37–71). In the first view, Jesus obviously uses the term in the most ordinary sense that "I am the son of human."[48]

Jesus' language here is hyperbolic or symbolic in ways that he exhorts them to be ready for harsh times ahead. We know clearly from Luke 22:49–50 that Jesus rejects violence.

47. Son of Man references in Ezekiel are as follows: "Son of man, I send you to the people of Israel . . . who have rebelled against me . . . You shall say to them, 'Thus says the Lord God'" (Ezek 2:3–4). Ezekiel continues: "And you, O son of man . . . shall set your face toward the siege of Jerusalem . . . and you shall prophesy against the city" (Ezek 4:1–7); "Son of man, you dwell in the midst of a rebellious house, who have eyes to see, but see not, who have ears to hear, but hear not" (Ezek 12:2).

48. Son of Man may mean just a human being as it is in Ps 8:5 of the Septuagint.

This view comes closer to understanding who the historical Jesus is given the fact that Jesus can be best understood as a Jewish prophet in first-century Judaism. What this means is his primary vocational identity is prophet for Israel; so, the second view is also very plausible. "The Son of Man came to seek and to save the lost" (Luke 19:10); similarly, "For the Son of Man also came not to be served but to serve, and to give his life as a ransom for many" (Mark 10:45; Matt 20:29). This "Son of Man must suffer many things, and be rejected by the elders and the chief priests and the scribes, and be killed, and after three days rise again" (Mark 8:31).[49] The third view of a future eschatological judge also appears in the Gospels (Mark 13:26; 14:62; Matt 24:30; Luke 18:8), but it does not seem to originate with the historical Jesus if his main identity is a reforming prophet for Israel working to change of lives here and now.

King of the Jews

The title "the king of the Jews" has something to do with the work of the historical Jesus since all the Gospels testify about his kingship in a certain way.[50] When the governor asks Jesus: "Are you the King of the Jews?" Jesus answers, "You say so" (Matt 27:11; Luke 23:3). In Mark as well, Jesus answers, "You say so" (Mark 15:2). In John's Gospel, Jesus not only affirms his kingship but states the clear purpose of his mission: "You say that I am a king. For this I was born, and for this I came into the world, to testify to the truth. Everyone who belongs to the truth listens to my voice" (John 18:37). Here Jesus' answer is seen as very political primarily because of this statement: "Everyone who belongs to the truth listens to my voice." If politics is

Walter Wink takes one step further by connecting the son of man with Jesus' authentic full humanity; Jesus is a model of faith and challenge to domination. See Wink, *Human Being.*

49. This prophetic referral is also found in the Gospels (Mark 2:10–11, 28; 8:31; 10:45; Luke 11:30; 17:22; 19:10; Matt 8:20; 11:19; 20:29; John 3:14–5).

50. According to a criterion of multiple attestation established in historical Jesus study, this title appears in more than two independent sources: Mark and John. Therefore, this title goes back to Jesus in some way. Moreover, this title conveys political implications about Jesus' work and does not seem to be invented by early Christians because it is not among the primary ones favored by them such as the Messiah or the Son of God. References about the king of the Jews in the Gospels: Matt 2:2; 27:11, 29, 37; Mark 15:2, 9, 12, 18, 26; Luke 23:3, 37; John 18:33, 39; 19:3, 19, 21. People mockingly hail Jesus as the King of the Jews (Matt 27:42; Luke 23:37; John 19:3), and the inscription of the charge against him also reads the same (Mark 15:26; Matt 27:37; Luke 23:38; John 19:19–21).

a partisan movement, Jesus is a politician for that matter because his speech motivates people to follow his cause of testifying to the truth about God. Jesus' kingship is subordinate to God, who is the true ruler on heaven and earth. His kingship is to establish God's rule, not his own rule. His method of kingship is not by weapons, but by the change of heart and mind, as Jesus' donkey-riding entry into Jerusalem insinuates (Mark 11:1–11; Matt 21:1–11; Luke 19:28–44; John 12:12–19). Jesus is not armed with weapons, but his symbolic act of entering Jerusalem with the applause of the crowds could be seen as very dangerous to political powers in Jerusalem because it may have stimulated a possible commotion during the Passover.

SUMMARY

With a careful study of both the historical Jesus and texts of the New Testament, we have explored the identity of Jesus with a focus on his birth, upbringing, and adulthood. Jesus grew up seeing his mother's sacrifice, hard work, and genuine spirit toward God. Jesus' view of family or community is shaped during this time when he sees all kinds of social ills and cruel powers of Rome and Jerusalem's collaboration with Rome. Jesus also seems greatly influenced by John the Baptizer's preaching and his lifestyle. After his teacher John the Baptizer was arrested, Jesus takes on full responsibility for his mission featuring the message of God's rule in the midst of "a kingdom of nobodies."[51] We have also seen that Jesus and John the Baptizer are not future- kingdom preachers but announcers of God's rule in the here and now. In God's time (*kairos*), present is future, and vice versa. To prepare for this rule of God, people have to seek God's way; that is what repentance (*metanoia*) means (Mark 1:14–15).

We also have explored the titles of Jesus. The historical Jesus is unlikely to have used all the titles in the New Testament. Nonetheless, Jesus' work is, directly or indirectly, connected with these titles as his followers relate to the significance of his work in their lives. Among other titles, the Son of God stands out, as Jesus is declared and exalted as the Son of God because of his faith and work. When early Christians claim that Jesus is the Son of God, they talk about Jesus' unique or special relationship with God. In the next chapter, we will see what Jesus primarily did in his life because of this particular relationship with God.

51. Crossan, *Jesus: A Revolutionary Biography*, 72.

Christianity is not taught
teach

4

The Work of Jesus

IN ORDER TO UNDERSTAND the work of Jesus, we must begin with his view of God in first-century Judaism. Jesus has a lot in common with other Jews and believes that there is one God of Israel, the only Lord (Deut 6:4–5), who must rule heaven and earth (Mark 1:14–15). Jesus even rebukes a man who calls him good teacher: "Why do you call me good? No one is good but God alone" (Mark 10:18). Likewise, Jesus inherits the great tradition of the double commandments (Deut 6:4–5; Lev 19:18). One of the scribes comes to Jesus and asks about the greatest commandment, and Jesus answers: "The first is, 'Hear, O Israel: the Lord our God, the Lord is one; you shall love the Lord your God with all your heart, and with all your soul, and with all your mind, and with all your strength.' The second is this, 'You shall love your neighbor as yourself.' There is no other commandment greater than these" (Mark 12:29–31; cf. Matt 22:34–40; Luke 10:25–28).

In Matthew, Jesus responds to those Pharisees who criticize his boundary-breaking fellowship with sinners and tax collectors: "Go and learn what this means, 'I desire mercy, not sacrifice.' For I have come to call not the righteous but sinners" (Matt 9:13; 12:7). Jesus quoted from Hosea 6:6: "For I desire steadfast love and not sacrifice, the knowledge of God rather than burnt offerings." In Matthew, Jesus is often addressed by people like this: "Have mercy on us, Son of David!" (Matt 9:27; 15:22; 17:15; 20:30–31). This means Jesus' primary work is understood as a prophet who advocates God's mercy toward those who are on the margin.[1] Matt 23:23 reads: "Woe to you, scribes and Pharisees, hypocrites! For you tithe mint, dill, and cummin, and have neglected the weightier matters of the law: justice and mercy and faith. It is these you ought to have practiced without neglecting the others." Justice without mercy is cruel or hollow; justice without faith is aimless or self-serving. Justice, mercy, and faith cannot be separated from each other.

In Matthew, Jesus emphasizes God's righteousness, which is fulfilled through Jesus' work. Even his baptism is to fulfill all righteousness (Matt 3:15). In teaching about God's world, Jesus asks to "strive first for the kingdom of God and his righteousness, and all these things will be given to you as well" (Matt 6:33). Through the parable of the vineyard laborers in Matt 20:1–26, Jesus teaches about the just and merciful God who equally provides all with daily food. God wants all laborers in the vineyard to get paid on the basis of a usual daily wage because all need basic necessities of life.

However, Jesus' view of God and Judaism is radically different from the contemporary Jews. First, he challenges a narrow application of the law that disregards the needs of everyday people, and corrects the view of God held by the Pharisees who demand a strict observance of the law regardless of circumstances. A test case for this is found in an episode of "plucking grain on the Sabbath" which appears in all the Synoptic Gospels (Mark 2:23–28; Matt 12:1–8; Luke 6:1–5). This episode is believed to come from the historical Jesus because it involves the cultural context of first-century Palestinian Judaism when this debate about the Sabbath is an issue. Moreover, I wonder if we can apply a criterion of embarrassment to Jesus' saying in Mark 2:27–28: "The sabbath was made for humankind, and not humankind for the sabbath." That is, when Matthew and Luke use Mark as a source, they seem to find this saying of Jesus embarrassing and omit it because their Jesus went too far, removed from the Jewish tradition according to which the Sabbath is kept for God; the focus of the Sabbath is God because "God blessed the seventh day and hallowed it, because on it

---

1. It seems that Jesus stands with Amos when he emphasizes mercy and justice of God. Amos rebukes the elites for their double standard about the day of the Lord: They wait for the day of the Lord while not seeking God's justice for the poor (Amos 5:18). He goes on to ask: "Is not the day of the LORD darkness, not light, and gloom with no brightness in it?" (Amos 5:20). Then Amos delivers the word of the Lord: "I hate, I despise your festivals, and I take no delight in your solemn assemblies. Even though you offer me your burnt offerings and grain offerings, I will not accept them; and the offerings of well-being of your fatted animals I will not look upon. Take away from me the noise of your songs; I will not listen to the melody of your harps. But let justice roll down like waters, and righteousness like an ever-flowing stream" (Amos 5:21–24).

God rested from all the work that he had done in creation" (Gen 2:3). It is very probable that the historical Jesus said this, even though it may be very embarrassing to late Evangelists such as Matthew or Luke because Jesus reinterprets the law and challenges a narrow application of the law. Jesus' point is human first and then the law, not vice versa. The Pharisees' point is the law first and then other matters, humanitarian or not. Jesus' interpretation of the law represents his view of God in that all creation must rest along with God on the Sabbath. If God only rests regardless of his creation, or if some elites only rest while others fall in danger, Jesus says it is wrong; the Sabbath was made for humans. In other words, there is no rest of God without the rest of all his creation. Otherwise, Jesus does not refute God's rest on the Sabbath. In some sense, Jesus' teaching of this kind reflects the teaching of Rabbi Hillel, a great teacher of the Torah just before Jesus, as written in Babylonian Talmud:

> Once there was a gentile who came before Shammai, and said to him: "Convert me on the condition that you teach me the whole Torah while I stand on one foot." Shammai pushed him aside with the measuring stick he was holding. The same fellow came before Hillel, and Hillel converted him, saying: "That which is despicable to you, do not do to your fellow, this is the whole Torah, and the rest is commentary, go and learn it."[2]

Here Hillel's point is not to deny the love of God but to emphasize the oneness of love that connects the love of God with the love of neighbor. Like Hillel, Jesus emphasizes the oneness of rest that connects the rest of God with all his creation. Otherwise, the law will be hollow or even become tools of control or abuse in the name of the law. The law should not be kept by blind faith but through "justice and mercy and faith" (Matt 23:23). Right after this episode of "plucking grain on the Sabbath" in Mark, Jesus heals a man with a withered hand on the Sabbath and asks the Pharisees, "Is it lawful to do good or to do harm on the sabbath, to save life or to kill?" (Mark 3:4). But the Pharisees were silent. Jesus' interpretation of the law and his view of God for that matter are not new, as Hillel, unlike Shammai, goes in that direction with his view of liberal interpretation of the Torah as we saw before. In a way, Jesus puts the law back in context where it serves God and all his creation.

2. Babylonian Talmud, Tractate *Shabbat* 31a. Another Rabbi Hillel's ethical teaching is worth stating here: "If I am not for myself, who will be for me? And if I am only for myself, then what am 'I'? And if not now, when?" (Pirkei Avot 1:14).

Second, Jesus also challenges the laws of retaliation (*lex talionis*)[3] stipulated in Exod 21:22–25. In first-century Palestinian Judaism, enemies are outside of neighborly love as reflected in Matt 5:43 ("You shall love your neighbor and hate your enemy"). But Jesus says, "Love your enemies and pray for those who persecute you, so that you may be children of your Father in heaven; for he makes his sun rise on the evil and on the good, and sends rain on the righteous and on the unrighteous" (Matt 5:44–45). Jesus breaks the customary understanding about the boundary of love; there is no limit. Moreover, enemies are to be loved not only because that is the job of children of God, but also because God is impartial to his love: the evil and the good, the righteous and the unrighteous. Jesus goes on to say, "For if you love those who love you, what reward do you have? Do not even the tax collectors do the same? And if you greet only your brothers and sisters, what more are you doing than others? Do not even the Gentiles do the same? Be perfect, therefore, as your heavenly Father is perfect" (Matt 5:46–48).

This kind of teaching is also found in the parable of the Good Samaritan (Luke 10:29–37). Just before this episode about the Good Samaritan, a lawyer comes to test Jesus and asks him about eternal life. Jesus answers him by asking him what the law says. Then, this lawyer answers him very well, citing the double love command in the law. Then, Jesus, recognizing his right answer, tells him: "Do this, and you will live" (Luke 10:28). The right answer is not enough for eternal life. Then, the lawyer gets to his main question: "Who is my neighbor?" (Luke 10:29). This is where Jesus begins his parable through which he redefines neighbor, not based on familiarity or blood or ideological ties but based on the need of a person. In the end of the parable, Jesus asks the lawyer, "Which of these three, do you think, was a neighbor to the man who fell into the hands of the robbers?" (Luke 10:36). Whereas earlier the lawyer asks who is my neighbor deserving such a love, Jesus shifts his question to a surprisingly new level and asks who should be neighbor to a person in need. The implication is that you are to be such a neighbor. Jesus seems to say: "Do not ask who deserves your love; if you become a neighbor to others, you are also loved by the other person; then

3. The interpretation of the laws of retaliation (*lex talionis*) in Exod 21:22–25 is complex since the text does not specify the law's exact application in the said situation. Scholarly interpretation is varied ranging from a literal understanding of equal retribution to a symbolic figurative understanding in that the teaching is about equal compensation (monetary) so that human life is valued, maintained, and recovered to the previous conditions. See Kim, "*Lex Talionis* in Exod 21:22–25," 99–112.

all become neighbors." This teaching resembles the one we saw in Matthew: Children of God must be impartial in showing the love of God, including to both the evil and the good, both the righteous and the unrighteous (Matt 5:44–45). Reluctantly or not, the lawyer has no choice but to answer Jesus correctly: "The one who showed him mercy" (Luke 10:37). Jesus says again, as he did earlier, "Go and do likewise" (10:37).

Third, Jesus also challenges the boundaries of people of God, including those between purity and impurity. By Jewish tradition, people of God are those who are bound by God's covenant, and because of that, they have to stay in the community. Here, God's covenant refers to a series of the covenants made with Abraham, Moses, and David in the Hebrew Bible; all the time, covenantal partners or beneficiaries are people of Israel. Even the new covenant of God in Jeremiah 31:31–34 is not for all people but for "the house of Israel and the house of Judah." This renewal of God's covenant requires people's hearts; the law will be written on their hearts: "I will be their God, and they shall be my people" (Jer 31:33). According to this covenant, Jews are only heirs of it. But Jesus challenges this notion that children of God are understood as the sole beneficiaries of God's love and care. The God in the historical Jesus is impartial like the sun rising on everybody. Likewise, Jesus has a different view of community and family: "Whoever does the will of God is my brother and sisters and mother" (Mark 3:35; see also Matt 14:46–50; Luke 8:19–25). How radical this is, compared with the traditional Jewish teaching! According to Jesus, family or community is not bound by blood or tradition, but it is newly formed by following God's will. This view of God is universal in its application; technically, anyone who does the will of God is God's child. Accordingly, Jesus breaks walls between purity and impurity and sits and eats with tax collectors and sinners, who are embraced in God's kingdom not because they are unfortunate but because they are also children of God.

With this above understanding of Jesus' context and view of God or first-century Judaism, we will zero in on three important theological phrases in the New Testament that can help us understand the work of Jesus: "the good news of God" (*euangelion tou theou*), "the rule of God" (*basileia tou theou*), and "the faith of Christ" (*pistis christou*). The first two primarily appear in the Synoptic Gospels, and the last one in Paul's undisputed letters. "The good news of God" is what Jesus proclaims at all risks; it is about God and God's good news. Jesus' proclamation of good news is about God's rule against Rome's rule. "The faith of Christ" is understood as

Christ's faith through which we get to see his works of God's righteousness. We will explore these in detail below.

PROCLAIMING THE GOOD NEWS OF GOD

Good news (*euangelion*) is a familiar term in the New Testament, but it is not so simple to understand. While it is used in Roman society and everyday lives, it is also used in the Gospels and Paul's letters, among others. Moreover, it is also the title of the four Gospels in the New Testament. Even within the New Testament this term is used with a variety of connotations. From the outset, "the good news of God" (Greek genitive phrase) must mean God's good news (subjective genitive). God is good news, not the emperor or human masters!

It is God's good news that Jesus takes, preaches, and lives out in his life, at the risk of his life and up to the point of death. Otherwise, it is not about Jesus at first hand. It is God's gospel that Jesus brings to the world. This is especially true in Mark, which begins with "the good news of Jesus Christ" (Mark 1:1). Jesus always points to God because God is sovereign and righteous. God is the initiator and source of the good news.

Paul also elevates God's good news, as he senses his apostolic call is for the good news of God (God's good news) in Rom 1:1. Later, he says "I am not ashamed of the good news; it is God's power for salvation for all" (Rom 1:16). Note here the good news is God's power for salvation for all. In that good news, God's righteousness is revealed (Rom 1:17). This means the sovereign God rules heaven and earth with peace and justice because God is righteous. In order for God's righteousness to be revealed, one has to live by faith! It is not free but can become a reality when it is followed through faithful living.

Overall, the good news (*euangelion*) in the Gospels and Paul's undisputed letters is very different from that in the Roman Empire. Whereas good news in the Roman Empire is made because of a violent victory, the good news of God is about justice and peace. The good news of Rome is propaganda that emphasizes one-man's rule at the expense of true justice, peace, or diversity in the world. In the Roman Empire, good news is that the kingdom of Rome prospers forever at the sacrifice of multitudes of the poor, slaves, and the marginalized. Indeed, this is not the good news for most people in the Empire because they are subjugated and compelled to follow the norm of hierarchical unity that all roads lead to Rome. It is good news for the elites or those on the top who enjoy the benefits of military victories. Otherwise, most people struggling with their daily lives are still hungry for the good news that they are liberated from all the shackles of violence and oppression. What follows is a detailed analysis of the good news.

The Good News in the Gospels

Mark begins with "the beginning of the good news of Jesus Christ" (Mark 1:1) and ends with the good news that women hear about the risen Lord (Mark 16:1–8). This inclusion of good news at the beginning and end of the gospel may be intended to mark the gospel as significantly different from what the people are used to.

Note here "the good news of Jesus Christ" is a genitive phrase, which connotes either the good news about Jesus or the good news that Jesus proclaims. But throughout the gospel, we know that Jesus proclaims the good news of God (Mark 1:14).[4] Moreover, Jesus asks to "believe in the good news" because God's time is "fulfilled, and God's rule has come near" (Mark 1:15). Jesus is a good news preacher and bearer of God's good news as he shouts out in Mark 1:15. The good news has to be trusted because of two reasons: "The time is fulfilled and God's rule has come near." Now is God's time that people have to respond to live with God's rule. There is no other time than now. In God's time, it is impossible to separate the present from the future, or vice versa. Because of this urgency of God's rule, Jesus asks people to change their hearts ("repent" *metanoeo* in Greek) to welcome God's rule in the here and now.[5] Also, Jesus praises the faith of his followers because of their work "for the sake of the good news" (10:29; see also 14:9). This good news must spread to all nations (Mark 13:10) because God's rule must be established everywhere.

Proclaiming the good news of God invites an unnecessary resistance from all sides of the powers and rulers in Jesus' time. Jesus knows about it, and he is deeply anguished. "I am deeply grieved, even to death; remain

---

4. The view that the gospel is about Jesus appears in Deutero-Pauline and Pastoral letters (2 Thess 1:8; 2:14; Col 1:5, 23; Eph 1:13; 3:6–7; 6:15, 19; 2 Tim 1:8, 10–11; 2:8). The author in 2 Timothy says Jesus is "my gospel": "Remember Jesus Christ, raised from the dead, a descendant of David—that is my gospel" (2 Tim 2:8). We will come back to this issue later when we deal with Paul's letters, Deutero-Pauline and Pastoral letters.

5. Crossan, *Jesus: A Revolutionary Biography*, 48, 56.

here, and keep awake" (Mark 14:34). Ultimately, it is his decision that he will continue to proclaim God's rule. "Abba, Father, for you all things are possible; remove this cup from me; yet, not what I want, but what you want" (Mark 14:36). Jesus renews the purpose of his life: "For the Son of Man came not to be served but to serve, and to give his life as ransom for many" (Mark 10:45). Here "his life" is not the price for the forgiveness of sins but the price of God's rule.[6]

In Matthew as well, the good news that Jesus proclaims is similar to Mark. It is about God's rule on earth: "Thy Kingdom come! Thy will be done, on earth as it is in heaven" (Matt 6:10). "Jesus went throughout Galilee, teaching in their synagogues and proclaiming the good news of the kingdom and curing every disease and every sickness among the people" (Matt 4:23). In God's rule, all are welcome, including little children and the poor (Matt 18:1–11; see also 25:31–46). This teaching about God's rule is well stated in the episode of the last judgment, and Jesus surprises his audience by reversing the expected result of the judgment: "Truly I tell you, just as you did not do it to one of the least of these, you did not do it to me" (Matt 25:45).

Jesus sends out his disciples for a mission of proclaiming the good news about God's rule (Matt 10:7). As a result, "the blind receive their sight, the lame walk, the lepers are cleansed, the deaf hear, the dead are raised, and the poor have good news brought to them" (Matt 11:5). The narrative of Matthew's Gospel follows the basic storyline of Mark, and Jesus is led to the cross because of his costly, dangerous preaching about God's rule in the here and now.

Luke also emphasizes a similar nature of the good news proclaimed by Jesus. The angel Gabriel brings "the good news of great joy for all the people" (Luke 2:10): The birth of a Savior, the Messiah, the Lord, in the city of David (Luke 2:11). But soon we know that this good news of Jesus' birth is because he "proclaimed the good news to the people" (Luke 3:18; see also 20:1). In a Jewish synagogue at his hometown, Jesus reads and interprets the scroll of the prophet Isaiah and proclaims the good news to the poor: "The Spirit of the Lord is upon me, because he has anointed me to bring good news to the poor. He has sent me to proclaim release to the captives and recovery of sight to the blind, to let the oppressed go free" (Luke 4:18; cf. 7:22; 8:1).

---

6. Dowd and Malbon, "Significance of Jesus' Death in Mark."

Salvation — to heal —

Jesus continues the work of the prophet Isaiah. His mission is to "proclaim the good news of the kingdom of God to the other cities also; for I was sent for this purpose" (Luke 4:43). Jesus came to seek and save the lost (Luke 19:10). Jesus trains his disciples and makes them fishers of people so that they continue his work. At the Lake Gennesaret when the crowds press in on him to hear "the word of God," Jesus teaches them and trains Peter on the sea (Luke 5:1–11). Jesus does not teach his word or wisdom, but God's word. Peter and others leave everything and follow Jesus: that is to preach the good news of God's rule or God's word. Notice here the crowds chase after Jesus to hear "the word of God," interchangeable with the good news of God. Jesus sends out his disciples for this mission of good news preaching (Luke 9:6): "They departed and went through the villages, bringing the good news and curing diseases everywhere." Like Mark, Luke also emphasizes the cost of this good news brought and proclaimed by Jesus the Son of God. The narrative of Luke follows the basic storyline of Mark and Jesus is led to the cross because of his costly, dangerous preaching about God's rule in the here and now.

Though there is not a single mention of good news in John's Gospel, we find a corresponding phrase "the Logos of God," understood as the word, spirit, or wisdom of God.[7] Jesus as the Son of God embodies and testifies to it. That is what John 1:14 must mean: "And the Logos became flesh and lived among us, and we have seen his glory, the glory as of a father's only son, full of grace and truth." The idea of incarnation here is hinged on "flesh," which represents this worldly place enmeshed with the physical and spiritual conditions of life on earth. That is, God's Logos is seen, felt, and experienced among people in this world. That is what incarnation means. Otherwise, the meaning here is not that God became Jesus; rather, Jesus is a revealer of God, but he is not God. He makes clear that his mission is to deliver God's Logos and to help his disciples and the world live in truth and sanctification: "I have made *your name* known to those . . . they were *yours*, . . . they have kept *your word*" (John 17:6; cf. 17:14, 17). Even before his trial before Pilate, Jesus is adamant about his mission: "I came into the world to testify to the truth" (John 18:37). He did not come into the world simply to die as if Jesus' death were necessary for the forgiveness of sins. Jesus' life is for the Logos of God, testifying to the truth of God, because God must

7. Luke T. Johnson states that there are ten "shared characteristics" in all four canonical Gospels, all of which basically look back to Jesus similarly with a focus on Jesus' faithfulness toward God's righteousness or God's kingdom. See Johnson, "Theology of the Canonical Gospels" 99–105. See also Kim, *Truth, Testimony, and Transformation.*

rule on earth. Like Jesus in the Synoptic Gospels, he sends out his disciples in farewell speeches (John 14–17): "As you have sent me into the world, so I have sent them into the world" (John 17:18). Like the cost of God's good news in the Synoptic Gospels, there is also a severe cost of testifying to the Logos of God. Jesus warns that his disciples will be hated by those who resist God's Logos or truth.

The Good News in the Undisputed Letters of Paul

Let me begin with Paul's gospel. First, it is not about "how I can be saved but about how we together can become children of God." This is the position of the so-called New Perspective on Paul, which emerged because of Krister Stendahl's monumental essay on Paul: "The Apostle Paul and the Introspective Conscience of the West."[8] In this essay, Stendahl questions the interpretation of Augustine and Luther, who project into Paul's mind their issue of feelings of internal guilt, and find the solution by making Paul a champion of Western Christianity, characterized by an individual justification by faith. Rather, Paul's major concern is: How can Gentiles join the children of God?

Second, Paul's gospel is not a law-free gospel but a law-discerning gospel. "Law-free" is a great distortion to an understanding about Paul's gospel because Paul never rejects the law. Paul upholds the law in Romans ("Do we then overthrow the law by this faith? By no means! On the contrary, we uphold the law" Rom 3:31). As a Pharisee, Paul knows God and his tradition very well. That is, the law itself is not wrong; it is God's gift and guidelines for his people. Simply, it is impossible for a well-trained Jew like Paul to think that the Jewish God can annul the law as if it had failed. Rather, Christ fulfills the law (Rom 10:4).

"Law-free" does not mean that Christians can be justified without the law or that they can do whatever they want because they are law-free. The truth is just the opposite. Paul's gospel is a law-discerning gospel. Here, the key word is discernment. His position seems to be that not all aspects of the law should be kept in all contexts. Rather, he distinguishes the fundamental law (such as the law of God, the law of the Spirit, or the law of Christ) from the peripheral laws such as circumcision especially when the gospel is preached to the Gentiles (for example: in Galatians). Paul's point is that the highest law is God's law and that God's righteousness must be revealed in

8. Stendahl, "Apostle Paul," 199–215; *Paul Among Jews and Gentiles*.

the world. Christ exemplified God's righteousness through his faith, which is the law of Christ. Followers of Christ must be led by the Spirit to imitate Christ. Paul's understanding about the law is summarized in Gal 5:14: "The whole law is summed up in a single commandment, 'You shall love your neighbor as yourself.'" While Jewish law is not rejected, its application must be based on this rule of love commandment. That is the law-discerning gospel.

Of course, Paul is concerned about Jews who do not come to believe that Jesus is the Messiah and their unenlightened minds in which they perceive that they are the sole heirs of God. Paul is also concerned about Gentile Christians who boast about their faith and their new membership in God's house while ignoring Jews or Jewish Law. In Romans, Paul warns them that God did not nullify his covenant with Israelites because they were faithless: "What if some were unfaithful? Will their faithlessness nullify the faithfulness of God?" (Rom 3:3).

Third, Paul's gospel is not about individual justification by faith in Jesus but about the individual/communal participation in Christ's faith for God's righteousness. Paul's faith needs Christ's faith. Simply put, Jesus' followers need the same faith as Jesus. That is what Paul confesses in Gal 2:20: "and it is no longer I who live, but it is *Christ who lives in me*. And the life I now live in the flesh I live *in the faith of the Son of God*, who loved me and gave himself for me" (my translation; italics are for emphasis). Paul says that it is Christ who lives in him and because of that, he says he lives in Christ's faith, not merely by his faith in Jesus. Here, the faith is Christ's and in fact this phrase ("faith of the Son of God") is a genitive phrase (*en pistei te tou huiou tou theou*). It is not by his own faith that Paul lives, but by Christ's faith that he lives. Furthermore, the preposition before faith is *en*, which is a plain sense of the English preposition "in" that denotes either place or "way" in a modal dative. Paul lives *in* Jesus' faith and he admires Christ's other-centered love and sacrifice, and because of that, Paul confesses that the driving force of his life is Christ and his faith. In this light, the translation of the NRSV in v. 20, "I live *by faith in the Son of God*" does not seem to convey what Paul emphasizes. Again, here we find a possible influence of the church that aims at the doctrine of justification by faith.

Fourth, likewise, Paul's gospel declares that what matters is not individual faith or righteousness but God's righteousness that is revealed through Christ's faith and for all who have faith (Rom 3:22). Paul's theology is theo-centric, not Christo-centric. It is God's righteousness that is manifested through Christ's faithfulness. God is righteous like the sun and allows sunshine on all; God wants his creation to live with lights. If people live with that, God's rule is actualized. In this regard, God's righteousness in Paul's letters is equivalent to a major theological term "God's rule" (*basileia tou theou*) in the Gospels.

Therefore, it is not an accident that Paul begins his letter to the Romans by making sure that he was called a slave of Christ, set apart for God's good news (Rom 1:1). That is, Paul's gospel begins with not Christ's but God's gospel (Rom 1:1), which concerns his Son. With the above understanding of Paul's gospel, let us see in detail what the gospel of God ("the good news of God") means. Paul says in Romans 1:1–2 that his apostolic call is for the "good news of God" promised by God through "his prophets in the holy scriptures." Here, the good news of God is God's good news (1 Thess 2:2, 8–9; 2 Cor 11:7; Rom 1:1; 15:16). God is the initiator, basis, hope, and sustainer of good news for his creation. God acts out his covenantal faithfulness through the descendants of Abraham and extends his steadfast love to all, Jews and Gentiles alike. This good news of God is carried out by Jesus Christ; that is called "the good news of his Son" (Rom 1:9), which means the good news proclaimed by his Son Jesus. Accordingly, "the good news of Christ" elsewhere in Paul's letters must be read as Jesus' proclamation of God's good news (1 Thess 3:2; 1 Cor 9:12, 2 Cor 2:12, 4:4, 9:13, 10:14, Gal 1:7, Phil 1:27). In this extension of God's covenantal love to Jews and Greek, Jesus the Messiah plays a decisive role in effecting God's good news through his radical faith and love of God and the world until dying on the cross. In Paul's terms, God's righteousness (Rom 1:18; 3:21–26; Gal 2:16–20) may be interchangeable with God's rule in the Synoptic Gospels. A snapshot of Paul's theology is found in Rom 3:22: "God's righteousness" (*dikaiosyne theou*) through "Christ's faithfulness" (*pistis christou*) for all who have faith. I will come back to the matter of Christ's faith later.

Because of this marvelous good news rooted in God and the Christly example of it, Paul succinctly confesses his faith and theology in Rom 1:16: "I am not ashamed of the good news because it is God's power for salvation. In it, the righteousness of God is revealed through faith." As many scholars readily point out, this is a thematic verse in Romans because there are crucial theological vocabularies that we have to interpret: the good news, God's power, salvation, righteousness, and faith. Though this is a thematic verse, its meaning is not self-evident. But my reading goes with the subjective genitive reading of "the good news of God," which Christ carries out (an objective genitive) as seen before. Paul is not ashamed of the good news because it brings God's power in the world through Christ's work (or faith), which then calls for participation of Jesus' followers, as Rom 3:22 put it: "God's righteousness through Christ's faith for all who have faith."

In Paul's letters, God's good news must be read in the context of the Roman Empire because people often hear in imperial propaganda that Rome brings peace and security. Paul and his communities lived in major Roman cities under the domination of Rome. This means that in their everyday lives, they struggle with a choice between God's way and Rome's way; there is also an ideological conflict between God's good news and Rome's good news. There is tension between the haves and have-nots. A variety of hierarchies is placed in all corners of the Empire: in gender relations or patron-client system, in view of Romans versus barbarians, in view of Roman citizens versus slaves, and even in a pantheon. In this kind of Roman world, when Paul talks about God's good news, power, righteousness, salvation, and Christ's faith, as we see in Rom 1:16, these terms (collectively) are most likely taken in different regards by each audience. It is God's good news, not Rome's good news, because Rome is known for its double character in terms of violent victory, silenced peace, and subsistent, servile bond between patrons and clients. It is God's power that equalizes all regardless of his/her origin and birth (see for example 1 Cor 26–30), not Rome's power that prioritizes on the basis of one's origin and birth. It is God's righteousness that gives a share to all, not Rome's justice that seeks to maintain the status quo of power and security. It is God's salvation for Jews and Greeks, not Rome's salvation that separates Rome's privilege from other subjects in the Empire. It is Christ's faith (the Messiah or the Son of God) that carries out God's good news for all at all risks, not the faith of Romans that only seeks their own interest.

A Shift of the Good News in Deutero-Pauline and Pastoral Letters

But we see a shift of the good news in Deutero-Pauline letters (Col, Eph, and 2 Thess) and Pastoral letters (1 Tim, 2 Tim, and Tit) of which Pauline authorship is disputed because their writing style, vocabulary, and theology are very different from Paul's seven authentic or undisputed letters.[9] In these writings, the good news is equated with Jesus.[10] So to speak, Jesus is

9. See Kim, *Theological Introduction*, 79–80, 104.

10. All references about the good news phrases in these later writings: Col 1:5, 23;

the good news; otherwise, there is no more emphasis on God's good news, and accordingly, Jesus Christ is viewed in terms of high Christology. Jesus is "seated at the right hand of God" (Eph 1:20–23; 4:1; 5:23). So Christ is "the image of the invisible God" (Col 1:15). Furthermore, Jesus became a universal ruler, head of the church (Col 1:18; Eph 1:22–23; 4:1; 5:23). He is "cornerstone of the household of God" (Eph 2:20).

The good news is also about what Jesus had done once and for all: a sin offering for the forgiveness of sins (Col 1:5, 23; Eph 1:13; 3:6–7; 6:15, 19; 2 Thess 1:18; 2:14; 1 Tim 1:11; 2 Tim 1:8, 10–11; 2:8). Christ offered himself once and for all "as means of redemption through his blood" (Eph 1:7; 2:13; 5:2; Col 1:14). Salvation is done (2 Tim 2:10), and the believer's role is to believe Christ's sin offering. Death was abolished (2 Tim 1:10). Not surprisingly, therefore, the good news is a glorious gospel about Jesus Christ, who was "raised from the dead, a descendant of David—that is my gospel" (2 Tim 2:8). The emphasis is on Jesus' resurrection and victory; the implication is all Jesus' followers will get from this benefit. Otherwise, there is no role of Christ crucified or Christ's faith that discloses God's righteousness in the world. That is why we rarely find the phrase the "good news of God" in these later writings.

Furthermore, the meaning of the good news in these later epistles differs from Paul's undisputed letters. As we saw, whereas the good news in Rom 1:1–17 is related to God and Jesus (God's good news in Rom 1:1, and "the good news proclaimed by Jesus" in Rom 1:9), the good news in these later epistles is used separately in the sense of knowledge; for example: "the gospel of your salvation" (Eph 1:13), "the gospel of peace" (Eph 6:15), and "the mystery of the gospel" (Eph 6:19). Whereas Paul's undisputed letters emphasize the link between God's good news and God's power for Jews and Greek, these later epistles emphasize a particular salvific knowledge about Jesus in terms of his sin offering for the forgiveness of sins.

This shift of the good news in these later writings is not a solitary one; it conjoins other shifts; for example, view of church, view of "the body of Christ," view of time (eschatology), and view of gender relation. In Paul's undisputed letters, the church is always God's church (1 Cor 1:2; 10:32; 11:22; 15:9; 2 Cor 1:1; Gal 1:13); but here, the church is now Christ's church (Col 1:18; Eph 1:22). Whereas in Pauline churches the church is egalitarian (Gal 3:28), and there is no hierarchy among different members in it because "you are *soma christou*" (1 Cor 12:27a), the church in later epistles

---

Eph 1:13; 3:6–7; 6:15, 19; 2 Thess 1:18; 2:14; 1 Tim 1:11; 2 Tim 1:8, 10–11; 2:8.

is organized hierarchically with the use of the body of Christ as a metaphor (Col 1:18; Eph 1:22–23; 4:1; 5:23), and now Christ is the head of the church. Women in the church are not equal with men anymore (1 Tim 2:11–15). Accordingly, in these later writings we do not find an emphasis of God's good news for which Jesus showed his faith. Whereas Jesus in the Synoptic Gospels or in Paul's letters, points his fingers to God, now in these later churches and epistles, people look at Jesus' fingers without looking at the God to whom Jesus points. All this has to do with the context of the later churches that become more conservative in their views of community and society. There is a different role of Christ between Paul's undisputed letters and Deutero-Pauline and Pastorals. See the Figure below.

Comparison of Christ in Paul's Undisputed Letters and Later Letters

Paul's Undisputed Letters	Deutero-Pauline and Pastorals
- Christ as power of God (1 Cor 1:24) - Christ as the foundation of the church (1 Cor 3:11) because of his faith - Christ as a model of faith: *pistis christou* as Christ's faith (Rom 3:21–26; Gal 2:16–20) - Christ's death as his love of God and the world (Rom 3:21–26; 2 Cor 5:17–20) - Christ's body as Christ's crucifixion (Rom 7:4; 1 Cor 12:27)	- Christ as the image of the invisible God (Col 1:15–18; 2:9; Eph 1:20–23; 4:1; 5:23) - Christ as the head of the church (Col 1:18; Eph 1:22–23; 4:1; 5:23) - Christ as the object of faith (*pistis en christo*: 1 Tim 1:16; 2 Tim 3:15; also Eph 3:12; Col 1:4, 23; 2:5, 7) - Christ as a universal ruler (Eph 1:20–22; 1 Tim 6:16; 2 Tim 2:12) - Christ's death as a vicarious suffering for the forgiveness of sins through his blood (Col 2:13; Eph 1:7) - Christ's body as the church (Col 1:18, 24; Eph 4:12; 5:23)

"The Kingdom of God" as God's Rule (*Basileia Toū Theou*)

"The good news of God" is what Jesus proclaims and is clarified with God's rule as he combines both of them in his message: "Now after John was arrested, Jesus came to Galilee, proclaiming *the good news of God*, and saying, 'The time is fulfilled, and *God's rule* has come near; repent, and believe in the good news'" (Mark 1:14–15). *Basileia tou theou* is translated as God's rule, which is different from the rule of emperor or human masters and requires a change of heart and a radical reconfiguration of powers and distribution systems aimed at all-inclusive good news of God. The usual translation of "the kingdom of God" does not convey this sense of God's initiative of love and justice. Moreover, the Hebrew equivalent *malkuth* has more to do with kingship than with space (1 Chr 29:10–12; Dan 4:3). The point is God must rule because God is good (character) and engages in the world (God's work). God is the true ruler and king on earth and in heaven. In other words, good news is that God must rule with justice and peace. However, proclaiming God's rule involves risks because Jesus' proclamation of God's rule is a direct challenge to the Roman government and to elites in Jerusalem and local provinces alike. Because of this challenge, Jesus is led to the cross. Moreover, Jesus' proclamation of God's rule is also different from other sectarian groups such as the Qumran community, where the marginalized people such as the lame and blind are excluded from the messianic banquet (1QSa 2:11–12). In contrast, Jesus advocates for them and invites and sits with the sinners and tax collectors (Luke 4:16; 6:20–22; 7:22; 14:13–24).

In fact, God's rule does not come into reality unless there is a change of heart for people. While God's rule is like the sunshine in that it radiates on all, both need cultivated ground so that it may bear fruit. Put differently, God's rule must be engaged with people and rulers in society. That is what Jesus hammers out in his proclamation: a change of mind and heart towards God's rule. The point is to return to God, not to the emperor or to human masters (cf. 1 Cor 7).

Why is Jesus so concerned with this particular message about God's rule? Why does he ask people to believe in the good news about God's rule instead of believing in himself (Mark 1:14–15)? Jesus' emphasis on God's rule is based on his own life experiences. In his upbringing and adult life, as we saw in the previous chapter, Jesus observes many social ills and crooked human hearts at personal or communal levels as well as at local, national, and international levels. Jesus may have lived an unfortunate life with misery and poverty. In Galilee, as Jesus works as a *tekton* (craftsman), he may have seen many people struggling to get their daily bread and water. He may have seen the gluttony of evil masters and the power of domination by elites from Jerusalem and Rome as well. This is the kind of environment in which Jesus grows up and thereby comes to devote himself to securing God's rule in the world.

With Jesus' life experiences in Galilee, we can hardly limit his proclamation about God's rule to be simply about the future or otherworldly in nature. Theoretically, Jesus could preach about the good news, saying something to the likes of "you will enter the future kingdom of God or be rewarded in heaven after you die." But if that was the basis for Jesus' preaching, his message about God's rule would not be a good solution to the people struggling with a lack of food and justice in the here and now. If that is what Jesus preaches, it means that God is not sovereign or almighty because no real change happens on earth in the lives of people. As Luke 4:16–30 shows, Jesus preaches with the Spirit about the real change of people's lives in the present. "The Spirit of the Lord is upon me, because he has anointed me to bring good news to the poor. He has sent me to proclaim release to the captives and recovery of sight to the blind, to let the oppressed go free, to proclaim the year of the Lord's favor" (Luke 4:18–19). God's good news needs God's rule set in place; it is not about a single change but about a change to everything in life, including political and economic aspects of life. There must be distributive justice to all in Jerusalem and Galilee because evil powers rule the world at the expense of the powerless. In the following, we will explore more about Jesus' work in terms of God's good news and God's rule in the New Testament.

Jesus' preaching of the good news is about God's rule, which is the translation of *basileia tou theou*. This phrase, often translated as "the kingdom of God," conveys a sense of both spatial and temporal meanings, hinged with the present or future kingdom of God. This phrase is certainly not out of thin air. The exact phrase "the kingdom of God" does not appear in the Hebrew Bible; but there are similar phrases "his kingdom" and "your kingdom" (1 Chr 29:10–12; Dan 4:3). The Hebrew word *malkuth* refers to a reign or rule; so the connotation is that God is the ruler of peace and justice, not human kings or masters. Considering the background of this phrase in the Hebrew Bible and the context of the Roman Empire, I prefer "God's rule" to "the kingdom of God." In fact, "the kingdom of God" is best understood as God' rule in Psalms of Solomon or in the Wisdom of Solomon 10:10.

In Mark, Jesus proclaims the good news of God concerning God's rule after John was arrested: "Now after John was arrested, Jesus came to Galilee, proclaiming *the good news of God*" (Mark 1:14). Jesus explains why people have to believe in the good news that he preaches; it is because "the time is fulfilled, and God's rule has come near; repent, and believe in the good news" (Mark 1:15). God's rule must be established in the here and now; God's time is fulfilled. There is no other time or place but in the right here where Jesus stands. Because of this urgency of God's rule, Jesus asks people to change their hearts ("repent" *metanoeo* in Greek) to welcome God's rule. That is "the good news of Jesus Christ" which means: the good news of God that Jesus proclaims. This good news must be spread to all nations (Mark 13:10). Jesus lived for this good news of God at all risks. It is his decision that he will continue this mission for God's good news: "Abba, Father, for you all things are possible; remove this cup from me; yet, not what I want, but what you want" (Mark 14:36).

In Matthew as well, Jesus proclaims "the good news of the kingdom" (Matt 4:23) by "curing every disease and every sickness among the people" (Matt 4:23) because God must rule on earth. In God's rule, God's will is done on earth ("Thy Kingdom come! Thy will be done, on earth as it is in heaven," 6:10). In God's rule, little children, the hungry and the poor should be embraced (Matt 18:1–11; see also 25:31–46). Jesus sends out his disciples for proclaiming the good news that God's rule has come near (Matt 10:7). What is happening because of the preaching of the good news of God's rule is listed in Matt 11:5: "The blind receive their sight, the lame walk, the lepers are cleansed, the deaf hear, the dead are raised, and the poor have good news brought to them." This good news of God's rule will be "proclaimed throughout the world" (Matt 14:14). Notice how the list in Matt 11:5 is a reversal/correction of a formerly dismal situation, perhaps as the people's life under the Roman Empire. Like Mark, Matthew also emphasizes the cost of this good news brought and proclaimed by Jesus the Son of God. The narrative of Matthew's Gospel follows the basic storyline of Mark, and Jesus is led to the cross because of his costly, dangerous preaching that God's rule welcomes all the marginalized in the here and now.

In Luke as well, Jesus proclaims "the good news of God's rule," saying he was "sent for this purpose" (Luke 4:43). In a Jewish synagogue at his hometown, Jesus reads and interprets the scroll of the prophet Isaiah and proclaims the good news to the poor: "The Spirit of the Lord is upon me, because he has anointed me to bring good news to the poor. He has sent me to proclaim release to the captives and recovery of sight to the blind, to let the oppressed go free" (Luke 4:18; see also 7:22; 8:1). At the Lake Gennesaret when the crowds press in on him to hear "the word of God" (interchangeable with God's good news), Jesus does not teach his word or wisdom, but God's word (Luke 5:1–11). For this teaching about God's word, Jesus' disciples left everything to follow him. Jesus sends out his disciples for this mission of preaching the good news (Luke 9:6): "They departed and went through the villages, bringing the good news and curing diseases everywhere." Like Mark and Matthew, Luke also emphasizes the cost of this good news brought and proclaimed by Jesus the Son of God. The narrative of Luke also follows the basic storyline of Mark, and Jesus is led to the cross because of his costly preaching about God's radical rule in the here and now.

Luke - 4 -

JESUS CHRIST'S FAITH (*PISTIS CHRISTOU*)

If we deprive Jesus of his faith, it is a great distortion to our understanding of Jesus, and it is like our making Jesus a Gnostic Christ that leads souls to heaven. How can we talk about his proclamation of God's rule without relating to his faith? How can we talk about discipleship without modeling his faith? How can we talk about his death apart from his faith? How can we talk about God's vindication of Jesus apart from his faith? Everything he speaks or does in the Gospels is part of his faith toward God, who is the source of life and good news for all.

It is Paul who emphasizes Christ's faith and uses the phrase *pistis christou* ("the faith of Christ") in Romans and Galatians. Most English translations render it "faith in Christ," interpreting this phrase as an objective genitive; that is believer's faith in Christ. This is very problematic. First of all, let me point out inconsistency of the translation in the NRSV. For example, *dikaiosyne theou* (Rom 1:17; 3:21–22) is translated as "the righteousness of God," which is neutral and good because it indicates that this phrase is a Greek indicative. It is the reader's job to decide the meaning of this genitive phrase (objective or subjective meaning). Likewise, *soma christou* is translated as "the body of Christ" (1 Cor 12:27 and elsewhere), and it is a neutral translation. But when it comes to *pistis christou* (Rom 3:22; Gal 2:16), it is not translated as the "faith of Christ," which is expected like two the previous genitive phrases. Instead, this genitive case is translated as "faith in Christ" each time. I simply point out the problem of the inconsistency of this Greek genitive case (see Excursus: Examples of inconsistent translations below). Perhaps I wonder if this is because the church is stronger than the academy or because doctrine is stronger than scholarship.

Second, *pistis christou* is meant to be a subjective genitive. A simple test case will be interesting. If Paul had meant the objective genitive meaning, he could have used a prepositional phrase (*pistis en christo*, found in Eph 1:15; 3:12; Col 1:4, 23; 2:5, 7; 1 Tim 1:13–16, 19; 2 Tim 3:15; 4:7) instead of a genitive phrase. *Pistis en christo* clearly means "faith in Christ";

Christ is the object of faith. In these later letters, the concept of faith also changes to a set of teaching or sound doctrine (1 Tim 1:3–5; 4:6; 2 Tim 1:5, 13). For example, faith here is to accept Christ's sacrifice that has to do with the forgiveness of sins (Col 1:14, Eph 1:7). Furthermore, in these letters, there is separation between faith and work (Eph 2:8–9; 3:12, 17; 4:5, 13; 1 Tim 2:10; 5:10; 6:8; 2 Tim 2:21; Tit 2:14). In Paul's undisputed letters, faith is first of all Christ's faith, and then believer's participation in Christ's death. In fact, both in the Gospels and Paul's undisputed letters, faith is directed to God, who is the source of life. Jesus proclaims God's good news and asks people to trust in God. Even in John's Gospel, Jesus says: "Believe in God, believe also in me" (John 14:1). It should be noted that "believe in God" is first and "believing in him" depends on God, the source of life. Jesus' point is like this: "Believe that I do the works of God."

Third, let me also point out that Rom 3:22 is a test case for Jesus' faith. In Rom 3:21 Paul initially states "the righteousness of God" that has been disclosed apart from law, and then he continues to talk about it: "the righteousness of God through *faith of Jesus Christ* for all who believe." If Paul had meant "faith in Jesus" for "faith of Christ," then he could have omitted the last part "for all who believe" because it is a needless repetition. So a more natural reading of Rom 3:22 is that God's righteousness is disclosed through Christ's faith and is now available for all who believe.

Fourth, if we examine Paul's overall ministry contexts and his entire letters, we are convinced that he elevates Christ's faith as a model of faith. He even asks his audiences to imitate Christ and die with him (1 Cor 4:16; 11:1; Rom 6:3–5). Paul's biggest concern is how both Jews and Gentiles become God's people together. The solution is Christ's example and his faith that collapses the walls between them. If we replace Jesus' faith with the believer's faith in Paul's letters, it is also a great distortion in our New Testament theology. In sum, Paul's theology will not be understood without talking about Christ's faith.

EXCURSUS: EXAMPLES OF INCONSISTENT TRANSLATIONS (ROM 3:21–25; GAL 2:20)

I will limit my observations to the problems of inconsistent translations in Rom 3:21–26 and Gal 2:20. The focus will be on *pistis christou* (faith of Christ) and we will see how different English versions translate it inconsistently compared with other genitive cases such as "the righteousness of God."

ROMANS 3:21–26

New Revised Standard Version (NRSV)

[21]But now, apart from law, **the righteousness of God** has been disclosed, and is attested by the law and the prophets, [22]**the righteousness of God** through **faith in Jesus Christ** for all who believe. For there is no distinction, [23]since all have sinned and fall short of the glory of God; [24]they are now justified by his grace as a gift, through the redemption that is in Christ Jesus, [25]whom God put forward as a sacrifice of atonement by his blood, effective through faith. He did this to show his righteousness, because in his divine forbearance he had passed over the sins previously committed; [26]it was to prove at the present time that he himself is righteous and that he justifies the one who has **faith in Jesus**.

The above bold-faced italicized phrases are genitive cases, whose use is varied depending on context: a subjective, objective, or an attributive genitive. The meaning must be decided within the literary and syntactical context. The most neutral translation of a genitive case is a two-noun phrase combined with "of"; for example, *dikaiosyne theou* as "the righteousness of God." The benefit of this translation is clear; by seeing the "of"-combined two-noun phrase, English readers will be alert and recognize this phrase as a genitive case, which means that the meaning must be deliberated in context. This in turn means that readers have to struggle to understand the true meaning of the genitive used here.

Actually, this kind of "of"-connected genitive translation is kept with most genitives in English bibles: the body of Christ, the love of God, the body of sin, the blasphemy of the Spirit, sin of the world, and etc. But when it comes to *pistis christou* ("faith of Christ"), most translations do not follow this trend or policy but take a stance to support the doctrine of justification by faith, translating it to an objective genitive meaning: "faith in Christ." English readers are simply deprived of an opportunity to ponder about the meaning of this genitive phrase because technically it can take either a subjective or genitive meaning. What Paul means must be decided by readers. In order to be consistent with the genitive phrases mentioned before, the NRSV should have translated *pistis christou* as "faith of Christ."

Common English Bible (CEB)

21But now **God's righteousness** has been revealed apart from the Law, which is confirmed by the Law and the Prophets. 22**God's righteousness** comes through **the faithfulness of Jesus Christ** for all who have faith in him. There's no distinction. 23All have sinned and fall short of God's glory, 24but all are treated as righteous freely by his grace because of a ransom that was paid by Christ Jesus. 25Through his faithfulness, God displayed Jesus as the place of sacrifice where mercy is found by means of his blood. He did this to demonstrate his righteousness in passing over sins that happened before, 26during the time of God's patient tolerance. He also did this to demonstrate that he is righteous in the present time, and to treat the one who has **faith in Jesus** as righteous.

Now compare the NRSV with the CEB. Noticeably, the CEB translates *dikaiosyne theou* to "God's righteousness," which is the translation of a subjective genitive. This is understandable because translators are confident that Paul means a subjective sense here. Exegetically, this translation should be better than "the righteousness of God," because Paul could mean such a subjective sense. At the same time, to give readers an opportunity to engage the "of"-connected phrase may be helpful, as we see in the NRSV. But when it comes to *pistis christou*, the CEB takes confusing stances. On the one hand, *pistis christou* in verse 22 is rendered a subjective genitive: "faithfulness of Jesus," which is good since Paul could have meant that. Yet, in the last part of v. 22, Greek does not have the object of faith, though the CEB adds "in him" before "faith." Exegetically, the object can be God or Jesus or something else. More surprisingly, *pistis christou* in verse 26 is rendered an objective genitive ("faith in Christ"), which is a real confusion to the readers. This sudden shift from a subjective to an objective genitive may be because of the doctrine of justification by faith.

New International Version (NIV 1984 version)

[21]But now *a righteousness from God*, apart from law, has been made known, to which the Law and the Prophets testify. [22]*This righteousness from God* comes through *faith in Jesus Christ* to all who believe. There is no difference, [23]for all have sinned and fall short of the glory of God, [24]and are justified freely by his grace through the redemption that came by Christ Jesus. [25]God presented him as a sacrifice of atonement, through faith in his blood. He did this to demonstrate his justice, because in his forbearance he had left the sins committed beforehand unpunished—[26]he did it to demonstrate his justice at the present time, so as to be just and the one who justifies those who have *faith in Jesus*."

Interestingly, the NIV is consistent in terms of the genitive translation to be understood in the objective sense: "a righteousness from God," "this righteousness from God," and "faith in Jesus." But this objective genitive translation is also problematic partly because English readers are deprived of the chance to engage with the genitives, mainly because it does not seem to accurately interpret what Paul means here. A majority of scholars believes that Paul is concerned not with "how can I be saved" but with "how can we, both Jews and Gentiles, become children of God." Therefore, Paul here refers to God's righteousness that embraces both Jews and Gentiles. However, the NIV makes it an objective genitive ("a righteousness from God" and "this righteousness from God"), which supports traditional atonement theories such as imputed or imparted righteousness (penal-substitution or satisfaction theory). Interestingly, the NIV changes the translation of *dikaiosyne* in v. 26 to "justice," instead of "righteousness" used in vv. 21–22. This change is due to the satisfaction theory of atonement; Jesus' death is to satisfy God's justice ("his justice") according to the satisfaction theory.

GALATIANS 2:20

With Gal 2:20, the NRSV is taken as an example of problematic translations since most English Bibles are not different from it.

NRSV

20and it is no longer I who live, but it is Christ who lives in me. And the life I now live in the flesh I live **by faith in the Son of God**, who loved me and gave himself for me.

"By faith in the Son of God" is the translation of *En pistei zo te tou huiou tou theou*. This translation is problematic. "*En pistei*" plainly means "in faith," so Paul seems to say "I live in faith." The Greek preposition "*en*" plainly means location, which is Christ; now this location is further clarified with a double genitive following: "faith of the son of God" (*pistei tou huiou theou*). Now, the exegetical question is whether this genitive is meant in an objective or subjective sense. This must be a subjective genitive in light of what he says just before this phrase. He says, "it is no longer I who live, but it is Christ who lives *in* me." Notice here the preposition "*en*" with Paul's living. Because Christ lives in him, he also can live in Christ. That is to say, "living in Christ" requires Paul to live in Jesus' faith. Paul seems to say he wants to be soaked with Jesus' faith, which is the location of his life and commitment. Paul is not emphasizing the believer's faith in Gal 2:20. Rather, Paul talks about the primacy of Christ's faith and sacrifice that he wants to imitate.

Summary of Christ's Faith

Christ's Faith as Obedience to the Will of God

Jesus obeys God's will that his righteousness is to be revealed in the world. Christ's faith is not a blind faith for God but an informed faith that seeks God's will. It is not the personal will of Jesus or of any tradition, but the will of God by which he puts his life at risk. Mere obedience does not help, but Jesus' informed genuine faith helps us to follow him because he discerns what God wants and what he has to do for it. Jesus understands the will of God that aims at an all-inclusive good news, embracing those who are not invited to regular social tables. This inclusive gospel of Jesus entails a heavy cost because his message is not welcomed by some. That is where Paul says in Rom 3:22 that God's righteousness (the subjective genitive) has been

NIV Bible

disclosed through Christ's faith (the subjective genitive) for all who have faith (this is also Christ-follower's faith just like the subjective genitive).

Christ's Faith as Embodiment of God's Good News

In a world where people in Galilee and elsewhere live in poverty and injustices due to leaders' corruption under the imperial domination, people need good news in their everyday lives so that they may live with God's love and justice. The fundamental claim Jesus makes is that God is the source of good news because God must rule in the here and now when pseudo-God or pseudo-prophets rampantly make their pies bigger at the sacrifice of the poor and the weak. No emperor or master can be the ruler, but only the God of peace and justice. Jesus points his finger to God, who must be worshipped and followed by all people. Jesus himself is not the source of life or good news; he is the Son of God who does the work of God at the risk of his life. He throws himself in the hands of the evil, not to defeat but to confront them and to ask God to take care of the world even after he is gone.

Christ's Faith as Other-Centered Love and Justice ☆ The Best

As John Dominic Crossan emphasizes, Jesus' work is summarized with "healing and a shared meal."[11] Jesus is not a mere romanticist who loves to talk about God or a mystic who lives away from mundane life. Jesus lives out his belief in his real life, befriending "unqualified" people and showing God's rule in his works and meals. Simply, his life is other-centered, and so he is a great paragon to follow. That is why early Christians exalt him, because God exalts him. It is like Jesus' saying that a seed must fall and die to bear fruit. Jesus "died for all" and therefore "all have died" (2 Cor 5:14). Here Jesus' death means his other-centered love and sacrifice. A Pauline moral lesson is that because Jesus dies, so all followers do as well. In that sense, no death, no life.

---

11. The quote is from Borg, *Meaning of Jesus*, 67. See also Crossan, *Historical Jesus*, 303–53; and *Jesus: A Revolutionary Biography*, 75–101.

SUMMARY

Jesus proclaims "the good news of God" (Mark 1:14); otherwise, he does not say he is good news nor does he proclaim about himself. Jesus' primary identity in the Gospels is the Son of God who does the works of God. It is God's good news that Jesus proclaims even at the risk of his own life. Otherwise, Jesus does not ask people to believe in him because he is the Messiah or the Son of God. Rather, he points his finger to God—the God of peace, justice, and righteousness. God is the reason or foundation of good news (a subjective genitive meaning) because God is righteous and steadfast in his love and care for his creation. The subject of good news is not Jesus but God. Jesus acknowledges that only God is good (Mark 10:18; Luke 18:19).[12]

Jesus brings the good news of God to the poor and the marginalized and advocates for them by healing them and challenging the leaders in society (Matt 18:1–11; 25:31–46; Luke 3:18; 4:16–30). Jesus works for them, and his work is not welcomed by some. Jesus' message and work of the good news of God is against all other kinds of good news that are against God's justice. The good news proclaimed by Christ is what Paul calls "the good news of his Son" (Rom 1:9), as Mark similarly does so when beginning his gospel: "The beginning of the good news of Jesus Christ" (Mark 1:1). Ironically, Jesus' proclamation of the good news of God is not well accepted even though the world needs it. While some accept and welcome it, others resist it because they fear that their status quo would be taken away. To those who are hungry in poverty and are thirsty for God's justice, Jesus' kingdom preaching becomes bread to them. They gladly hear and follow Jesus because they see the work of God through him. But to those in power, it becomes an uncomfortable truth that challenges their behaviors and ambitions to accrue more. This good news of God proclaimed by Jesus demands a change of heart so that God's rule may be established in the midst of people's lives. A change of heart is what repentance (*metanoia*) means. It requires people, rulers and powers to follow God's way—a way of justice and mercy, turning away from their self-seeking interests. Repentance here is not limited to individual matters only; rather, it is a total change of mind and heart that seeks God's way in personal and public life. Otherwise, if Jesus had talked about some sort of an apolitical, otherworldly utopia, he would not have been executed by Rome on the cross.

12. In contrast with Mark, Matthew finds Mark 10:18 uncomfortable and changes it to "Why do you ask me about what is good?" (Matt 19:17). Historians believe that Jesus could speak this saying of Jesus in Mark 10:18.

5

The Death of Jesus

JESUS DID NOT COME simply to die on the cross. He was supposed to live a good life without a tragic death on the cross. In other words, death is not the goal of his life, as opposed to the popular Christian belief that "Jesus came to die for us." As we have seen in the previous chapter, Jesus came to proclaim God's good news (*euangelion tou theou*), which is about God's rule (Mark 1:14–15), to testify to the truth (John 18:37), and to show God's righteousness through his faith (Rom 3:22). Jesus did not come to die for us but came to show who God is. The result is his death on the cross, a tragedy that cannot be romanticized or spiritualized for whatever reason. Jesus knew he would be killed if he continued his work.

Therefore, a mere emphasis on Jesus' death or blood without looking at the historical context of his death is not only unrealistic, but keeps us from seeing both his love and passion for the world, and the ugly faces of the evil that are accountable for his death. If Jesus' death is read only as a vicarious sin offering, it is like suffocating Jesus' testimony to God's justice in the world. People often watch Mel Gibson's movie *The Passion of the Christ*, weep, and thank Jesus because he was punished instead of them. This kind of penal substitution theory of atonement blinds people from seeing the evil system or powers held accountable for Jesus' death. If Jesus' death were God's plan, then how can one account for the Gospel of Judas? In it, Judas Iscariot is praised because he helps Jesus to die so that salvation is complete. So the essential question before we explore the meaning of his death is *why* he was put to death. We care about Jesus' death not because he *died* but because he died *tragically* because of his poignant teaching and dangerous acts toward the power center of Jerusalem and Rome. Crossan's words are helpful here: "If Jesus had lived, did everything we know he did, and just died in his own bed, he must have been talking only about the interior life, because Rome is not paying attention, no one is bothered by it."[1] So the relevant questions are: Why was he put to death? What does his work have to do with his death? These questions are crucial not only to understanding the death of Jesus but also to constructing New Testament theology.

THE CONTEXT OF JESUS' DEATH

With this primary context of Jesus' death, we can think of a few surrounding contexts. First, there is a context of family in which Jesus grows up and his identity is formed. Given the devastation of village life in Galilee due to the religious, political corruption, and chaos, coupled with his irregular family of a single mother and other siblings, Jesus' childhood seems to endure waves of turmoil. For example, the village people are suspicious about his identity because of his poor family background (Jesus being a carpenter). Jesus is influenced by his impoverished upbringing to become a deep thinker and visionary.

Second, Jesus, as a deep thinker, cannot turn a blind eye to the social ills and ruins of the local economy. When villages are ruined with lots of destitute tenants, when the legions of the Roman army are stationed to control Galilee and elsewhere, when local elites and authorities in Jerusalem do not care about people, and when everyday people do not know what to do, we cannot imagine a silent Jesus who opts for inaction.

Third, concerning the religious, political context, Jesus cannot tolerate the very powers of evil coming from people.[2] The problem of evil does not lie in otherworldly contexts, but it is a human problem in that people do not seek God's righteousness (Matt 6:33). Jesus is supposed to know very well about his Jewish tradition, according to which the God of Israel is the God of the universe and the Lord is sovereign and has to rule with justice. Otherwise, no human masters, kings, or even the Jerusalem Temple can

---

1. Crossan, *Message of Jesus*, 54.

2. Borg, *Jesus: A New Vision*, 79–124. Borg puts Jesus in social cultural context where Jesus works as a Spirit person deeply committed to the work of God as a healer and sage.

replace such an almighty God. All in all, Jesus seems to know very well whom or what he has to face in order to restore God's rule here and now.

In sum, the context of Jesus' death cannot be singled out to one particular element or moment. Rather, it involves multiple contexts as we briefly saw above. Therefore, Jesus' death must be understood in terms of all of these complexities. Because of his new vision about God's rule, advocacy for the less fortunate and the marginalized and relevant message of a challenge to political, religious leaders, Jesus invites unwanted oppositions from those leaders. He could see danger coming his way. But I suppose the most decisive cause of Jesus' death would be his challenge to the Jerusalem Temple, including the powers in Jerusalem and Rome. This view makes sense, given the significance of the temple as a religious, political, and economic center in Roman Palestine.

The simple truth is that if one simply talks about the love of God without challenging the powers or people, he/she would not be in danger. A more recent example would be helpful. If Martin Luther King, Jr. had only talked about the love of God for all without challenging racial discrimination, economic injustices, or other forms of evil in society, he most probably would not have been assassinated. As for King, God's love means that all are equally loved and respected in their identity as God's creation. But in order to make such a beloved society, people have to change. But some do not want to lose their privileges. That is where the trouble emerges with King's speech and action. Likewise, if Jesus had only spoken about the apolitical, innocuous good news of God, as we hear today from many pulpits, he may not have been put to death. In Borg's term, "the domination system killed Jesus as the prophet of the kingdom of God."[3] Jesus was killed because he challenged the dominant system.

THE REASON FOR JESUS' DEATH

With the above contexts of Jesus' death, we will zero in on the reason for Jesus' death, which is distinguished from the meaning of Jesus' death. If Jesus' message had been accepted by people and authorities in his time, he would not have been executed on the cross. In the Synoptic Gospels, Jesus begins his public ministry by proclaiming God's rule. He advocates for the most unfortunate (prostitutes, tax-collectors, sinners, outcasts), calls disciples with a multitude of followers for his ongoing mission, and challenges the

3. Borg, *Meaning of Jesus*, 91.

status quo of society with a new vision of God's time here and now. Because of his work, Jesus is opposed, hated, and put to death by Pilate. This logic is also applied to John's Gospel, though the language of John is much different from the Synoptics. In John, Jesus does the works of God as the Son of God. Because of that, he is opposed and eventually put to death on the cross. The raw fact about Jesus' death seems clear according to the story of the Gospels: on one hand, Jesus dies honorably before God because he does the works of God; on the other hand, Jesus is put to death by the authorities because of his challenge to the status quo of society.

In Paul's undisputed letters, he seems to know why Jesus was put to death. Jesus' faith (*pistis christou*) led him to his death because of his love of God and the world. To show God's righteousness in the world, Jesus had to confront powers, advocating for the weak and the powerless. This idea is gained primarily from Rom 3:21–26 and 1 Cor 1–4 among other places. In the former, while emphasizing the link between God's righteousness and Jesus' faith, Paul talks about Jesus' death as *hilasterion* (atoning sacrifice), which is a result of his faith that demonstrates the radical light of God like the dazzling sun in the world. In the latter, Paul understands Jesus' death as the wisdom and power of God not because he simply died but because he challenged the wisdom and power of the world. Paul says in 1 Cor 1:28–30, God chose the weak and the most unfortunate in the world. Jesus served this cause of God's vision of radical egalitarian community in his life. That is what led him to his death. Otherwise, the vicarious death of Jesus is not Paul's idea.

While the reason of Jesus' death can be understood in terms of a gradual process because of his message and action, it can also be understood in terms of a decisive moment in his life. Bluntly, it is an episode about his Temple disruption as testified in all the Gospels (Mark 11:15–17; Matt 21:12–13; Luke 19:45–46; John 2:13–15).[4] However, I do not suggest that this event of Jesus' Temple cleansing is the only decisive reason by which he is sought to be killed as some scholars reason,[5] but what I am saying is

4. While in John timing of the Temple cleansing happens early in his public ministry, in the Synoptics it happens later in his ministry days before his crucifixion.

5. For example, John Meier thinks that Jesus confronts priests as he tries to reform the corrupt Temple. Similarly, E. P. Sanders thinks that Jesus' cleansing act is seen as dangerous to the Temple authorities because his behavior in the Temple can be seen as a protest against Rome. Meier, *Marginal Jew*, 207–14; Sanders, *Historical Figure of Jesus*, 272–73. See also Grant, *Jesus: An Historian's Review of the Gospels*, 153.

that this event serves as a kind of climactic, symbolic act that represents his passion and vision for God's rule in the world in the here and now.[6]

With the above caution about the decisive reason for Jesus' death, I consider Jesus' cleansing of the Temple to be a watershed moment because he challenges the very system of the Temple and the imperial connections with it.[7] Everybody knows that the Temple is so holy that nobody can disrupt its activities from the perspective of religious elites and priests. But Jesus demonstrates that the Temple is malfunctioning as it should be "a house of prayer for all nations" (Mark 11:17; see also Isa 56:6–7), which means that it should be a sanctuary for all people who need recovery of their status from social ills.[8] Jesus seems to point out a few problems here at the Temple. First, there are people who take advantage of this opportunity to sell animals to those who did not prepare for an offering. Second, those who buy animals are also driven out with the sellers. This suggests that these people are also problematic in that they did not prepare their hearts when they came into the Temple, thinking only about a market in the Temple area, and believing that all things will be taken care of if they do all the rituals. Third, more specifically, the Temple does not function as it should, as a place of sanctuary (protection), a place of recovery from former ruins or damage in their lives. That is why Jesus emphasizes that it is a house of prayer, and not a "market" (*emporium*) (John 2:16). Fourth, there is big power behind this market: priests and other religious leaders who take advantage of this system. So Jesus' act of cleansing the Temple by overturning the tables of the money changers and driving out those who sell and buy is a direct challenge to those who are in power. In this regard, "a den of robbers" (Mark 11:15–18; Matt 21:12–13; Luke 19:45–46; see also Jer 7:11) may refer to those who are involved in the exploitation of the poor and ordinary. "And when the chief priests and the scribes heard it, they kept

---

6. Adele Reinhartz disagrees with the above traditional historical view of Jesus' cleansing of the Temple linked with Jesus' death because the canonical Gospels do not specify such a link; rather, the real element by which Jesus is sought to be killed is rather his popularity or teachings about the Kingdom of God. See Reinhartz, "Temple Cleansing and the Death of Jesus," 100–111.

7. My reading on the motive of Jesus' disruption of the Temple is different from others. N. T. Wright sees this act of Jesus as a symbolic gesture that Jesus replaces the Temple. See Wright, "Mission and Message of Jesus," 32–52.

8. I do not think Jesus intends to replace the Temple with himself. What he intends to do is to reform it. Jesus' act may be "a symbolic destruction of the Temple." See Crossan, *Message of Jesus*, 75.

looking for a way to kill him; for they were afraid of him, because the whole crowd was spellbound by his teaching" (Mark 11:18).

As we see here, what really enrages Jesus is not simply the market incident or dishonest merchants but the function of the Temple: a place of protection, promise, care and support, and restoration of people's lives. On the one hand, there are abusers (sellers, chief priests, and other leaders) of the system; on the other hand, even those who buy animals are not prepared for the ritual at Passover because of their easy-going attitude that a surrogate animal is enough. The question is, however, as to whether this fury of Jesus is purely religious. The answer is no, because Jesus seems to know very well how his act of Temple cleansing would send out political repercussions to the authorities in Jerusalem, including chief priests and the Sadducees. Moreover, as we explored the identity and work of Jesus in chapters 3–4, politics is hardly separated from the economy or religion in this time. It is a known fact that the Temple and Jewish authorities are maintained because of their cooperation with the Roman imperial authorities represented by Pilate.[9] In other words, Jewish authorities do not want fission of their powerbase or collapse of the status quo because of Jesus' challenge to the Temple and its authorities. There will be a domino effect. If the Temple authority collapses, the next thing is the very challenge to the powers of Jerusalem and Rome. Since Jesus already made his work and name known before he came to disrupt the temple, he appears to be the object of scrutiny from the central powers. His bold proclamation about God's rule is a serious challenge to both the powers of Jerusalem and Rome. Now Jerusalem authorities feel the nerve directly under their skin. Remember it was Passover when Jesus did this act of cleansing. Mobs and other crowds who follow Jesus could instigate mass protests. So there is a fear factor going on with the chief priests and the Pharisees: "So the chief priests and the Pharisees called a meeting of the council, and said, 'What are we to do? This man is performing many signs. If we let him go on like this, everyone will believe in him, and the Romans will come and destroy both our holy place and our nation'" (John 11:47–48). This is where the high priest Caiaphas suggests the interesting idea of a vicarious death for Jesus, in order to achieve a double goal: prevent Roman destruction and secure the unity of Israel. "But one of them, Caiaphas, who was high priest that year, said to them, 'You know nothing at all! You do not understand that it is better

9. Borg, *Meaning of Jesus*, 90.

for you to have one man die for the people than to have the whole nation destroyed'" (John 11:49–50).

In sum, we can conclude that the death of Jesus is a result of his costly preaching about God's rule, which challenges both the Roman and Jewish authorities.[10] Jesus came not to die but to testify to the truth of God (John 18:37).

THE MEANING OF JESUS' DEATH

In general, we can distinguish between the reason/cause of Jesus' death and the meaning of it. Whereas the former concerns the work of the historical Jesus, the latter concerns the significance of his death for his followers. But strictly speaking, such distinction is arbitrary because the historical reason of Jesus' death also carries a meaning that is necessary to readers. For the meaning of Jesus' death in terms of the historical reason, we may focus on Jesus' character and works which led him to the cross. So readers are challenged to live like Jesus in his risk-taking ministry. Nothing could block him from teaching about God's love, justice, and peace: political or religious powers, even death. His death teaches us that living in the truth is difficult, thorny, and costly. Yet it is worth living that way because it is the way of God that seeks life and light for all. His death is a result of his commitment to God's good news about God's rule.

However, at the same time, Jesus' death must be considered a tragic event. The lesson is that evil must be judged; those who are accountable for his death are to be condemned and judged. They have to repent! Jesus' death was not planned by anybody, God or Jesus himself. In that sense, Jesus' death is an unwanted result! It is a shame to those who perpetrated this. But from Jesus' perspective, he does not avoid an impending death-like punishment from those who oppose him. In sum, from Jesus' death we learn his love for God and the world and God's judgment about evil.

The above historical meaning of Jesus' death is attested in the canonical Gospels and Paul's early letters (the seven undisputed letters). But if we read later writings such as Hebrews, Deutero-Pauline or Pastoral letters, the historical meaning of Jesus' death begins to fade away. Instead, Jesus' death is de-historicized in ways that his death matters only because of its

10. I do not agree with Raymond Brown who vehemently argues that it is the Jewish leadership (Sanhedrin) that puts to death Jesus by pushing Pilate to follow their wish. Brown, *Death of the Messiah*, 1:20–82.

salvific atonement, apart from what caused him to die. Such is the language of Hebrews that relates Jesus' death to the forgiveness of sins.

Atonement in the Hebrew Bible

In fact, the meaning of Jesus' death in the New Testament is not so simple because different authors/communities in the New Testament interpret Jesus' death differently and also because we too can interpret it differently. The predominant image or meaning of Jesus' death reflected in the New Testament comes from rather a complex, technical word called "atonement,"—borrowed from the Hebrew Bible, the plain sense of which is reparation for an offense. In the Hebrew Bible, atonement is made for individuals or the whole community (Israel). Throughout the year, the priests make atonement for individuals by a sin offering (where blood is involved). On the Day of Atonement (*Yom Kippur*), the high priest makes "atonement for the people of Israel once in the year for all their sins" (Lev 16:34; see also Lev 16; 23:26–32).

Atonement involves several things. First, the priests do this job on behalf of people. They are mediators between God and people, making sure that people are continually in good relationship with God. They are privileged to do such an important work for people and yet are greatly responsible for making atonement for people so that they can live holy individually and communally. This atonement is between God and people, but its effect must be on personal and communal lives. In other words, there cannot be a separation between reconciliation with God and reconciliation with people. The love of God is to be maintained with the love of neighbor. Second, people have to bring sacrifice objects for their sins to the priests. This means they have to acknowledge the need for reparation or mending their relationship with God and their neighbors. In other words, they must come with broken hearts because of their particular sins.

Third, atonement needs the blood and sacrifice of animals. The meaning of the blood-sacrifice is complex; it may mean scapegoat, a cost of reparation, or propitiation.[11] The scapegoat idea is certainly found with the azazel tradition on the Day of Atonement when a goat is sent out into the desert carrying the sins of people. While this goat is not killed but sent out to the desert, on the Day of Atonement, bulls and goat are sacrificed. At the last procedure of the event, this goat is sent out so that, symbolically or

11. For more, see Westbrook and Lewis, "Who Led the Scapegoat," 417–22.

literally, the sins of people are taken away. This sending out of a goat cannot be understood apart from the earlier acts of sacrifice done by the priest because this final act is the confirmation of what happened earlier. That is, people repent because of animal sacrifice and the entailing blood. Then the final act of sending out a goat can be understood symbolically; it is the confirmation of reconciliation or reparation between God and people because of that sacrifice and people's repentance. A cost of reparation is for getting relationships back to God. If damage is done in the community, there must be a measure of reparation to the victims. It can be monetary compensation or anything that can help to recover the victims from the damage. If damage is done between God and people because of their sins, the only way they can restore their relationship with God is to repent of their sins and do right measures in the community. Otherwise, as we saw even in the idea of a scapegoat, the sacrifice itself cannot be a perfect atonement. The death and blood of animals in sacrifice must be understood theologically and symbolically with a reminder that what must be truly sacrificed are not the animals but the people.

Atonement and Jesus' Death

In light of the Hebrew Bible's understanding about atonement, how can we relate Jesus' death to atonement? Was Jesus punished instead of people (penal substitutionary theory of atonement)? Or, is Jesus' death placating God's wrath (propitiation theory)? Does Jesus' death satisfy God's justice (satisfaction theory)? Or, does it have to do with a ransom paid to the devil (ransom theory)? Or, is Jesus' death a moral sacrifice that challenges Jesus' followers so they may live like him (moral sacrifice theory)? Each of these views has merit but is only partial. The merit of penal substitution or propitiation theory is to remove guilty feelings and to recover a sense of re-connection with God. So this meaning is valid for an individual who suffers from isolation due to guilt or sins. Likewise, satisfaction theory explains God's justice and the importance of a price of justice for sinners. Ransom theory emphasizes the freedom of salvation from the grips of the devil. All of these atonement theories, however, were developed a long time after Jesus' life, and all of them share a common element in that they fail to grapple with the death of the historical Jesus.

Except for moral sacrifice theory, all the atonement theories above tend to ignore the power of the evil or violence done to Jesus. Human violence and evil must be condemned because Jesus was sacrificed by the powers and authorities. It should not happen to anyone, including Jesus, because violence is harmful. In this sense, Jesus' death itself is not something that can be appreciated. Often, people sing the precious blood of Jesus as if the blood of Jesus is a necessary criterion for salvation. As I wrote elsewhere, "Protestant teaching and preaching most frequently tends to advance a single view of Jesus' death: The 'penal substitution' theory. This position holds that 'Jesus died, instead of me, because of my sin. Jesus was punished in my place. As a result, Jesus is not punished, and I am saved once and for all.'"[12] Unfortunately, this position is often viewed as the only correct one, but it is also a very limiting one. When exploring the concept of atonement, it is risky to emphasize any one interpretation of Jesus' death, particularly the penal substitution theory, to the exclusion of all others.

The danger of a one-sided view of atonement is seen in the movie *The Passion of the Christ*, which reflects Mel Gibson's Jesus—his passion for a "Western" Jesus, who comes to die and is punished instead of "me." The movie begins with a quote from Isaiah's Suffering Servant Song: "But he was wounded for our transgressions, crushed for our iniquities; upon him was the punishment that made us whole, and by his bruises we are healed" (Isa 53:5). In fact, within the literary context of Isaiah, the figure of the suffering servant does not refer to an individual, but to Israel. Taking the theme of the suffering servant and applying it to Jesus, Gibson colors his "Jesus" with "substitutionary death" (the so-called penal substitution theory) and much violence in the movie. The movie is full of unnecessary, exaggerated torture with little information about the cause of Jesus' death in a historical sense. Why is there so much violence to Jesus? Bluntly, the question is: Who brought Jesus to death? Let us get straight to the cause of Jesus' death. In fact, if Jesus' preaching of the kingdom of God (*basileia tou theou*) had been successful or his mission had been accepted by the people in his time, he would not have been killed. All the gospel stories present the cause of Jesus' death as the culmination of what he said, did, and performed. In other words, his message and deeds were dangerous for some people. That is why he was opposed and executed by those who resented his message. Jesus' passion for God's love and justice got him killed.

Even in our world today, there are much unjust and needless suffering. God does not want us to be tortured. Jesus' is a type of the most vicious and unjust suffering and death. This way of reading Jesus' death is certainly

12. Kim, "Jesus' Death in Context," 12–13.

plausible and one important avenue to look at the history and meaning of the event.

In fact, the cause of Jesus' death could be constructed in many different ways, as the Four Gospels themselves in the New Testament testify. In Luke, Jesus' work as a prophet provokes enemies' anger. Jesus dies as a martyr, not as salvific atonement or substitutionary death at all; his radical message of justice and egalitarianism led to the cross. In Matthew and Mark, Jesus' death is pictured as a good sacrifice for "others." Here a caution is that the sacrifice of Jesus does not automatically mean the penal substitutionary death of Jesus. On one hand, the meaning of Jesus' death can be constructed in the context of different communities behind the Gospels. On the other hand, apart from the later communities' meaning of Jesus' death, the cause of Jesus' death can be constructed in a more historical sense, which involves the analysis of all aspects of life in the world ranging from politics to economy to religion. If we continue to discuss the cause and meaning of Jesus' death, we will be faced with the question of "what we should do" today. The biggest problem of Gibson's movie is that it seems to condone the social, political evil of violence and injustice, and be blind to the massive power of evil evident in such atrocious, unspeakable torturing and murdering under the cover of a divine plan. The deters us from being able to reflect on how the power of evil can manifest in the form of violence or politics in our daily lives today. The movie's impression was that "the more violence on Jesus, the holier Jesus is, and the more thankful Christians feel because 'our sins are paid back.'" But again, in other contexts that I mention here, the message of the movie takes a one-hundred-eighty-degree turn: "There should not be another Jesus of unjust suffering and death in this world." Such atrocious, senseless violence and suffering must disappear in our world. Of course, this movie is not based on the historical Jesus or on critical scholarship, but based on a particular theological story interpreted and directed by Gibson who follows a specific understanding of the meaning of Jesus' death. If someone too quickly responds to this movie as if this were history *per se*, he or she evidently does not distinguish between history and theology.

Even this theological story, which portrays a vicious or violent role for the Jews and the Romans, should not be generalized to all Jews in history. Of course, not all Jews were involved in accusations against Jesus. There were good and faithful people like Mary, Jesus' mother, Mary Magdalene, disciples, and many nameless women who followed Jesus. Also, we cannot simply equate Jewish ancestors with Jewish people today. So if any person does not distinguish between individuals and community, and between the past and the present, that person brings in impending dangers. I reject such a naïve thinking or attitude about the gospel story.

As a whole, this movie must be viewed critically and/or with multiple dimensions of texts involving Jesus' life and death. Again we must know that penal substitution theory is conducive to ethical blindness, especially in the context of so much violence and war. Rather we have to affirm the value of life from the image of the cross. Why do we not see the evil powers at work in Jesus' time and today? How can we live in the midst of unjust, unwanted, innocent sufferings of so many people?[13]

JESUS' DEATH AND THE FORGIVENESS OF SINS

Let us take another angle of the meaning of Jesus' death with a focus on the language of "the forgiveness of sins."[14] In the Synoptic Gospels, Jesus' death is not directly related to the forgiveness of sins, which happens through baptism or repentance. John the Baptist proclaims a baptism of repentance for the forgiveness of sins (Mark 1:4; Luke 3:3) and people come to be baptized and are forgiven. In Mark, Jesus' death raises a challenge to the

---

13. Likewise, "the body of Christ" in 1 Cor 12:27 as a metaphor can be read as a broken, crucified body of Christ, which then can be identified with all forms of broken bodies in the world, especially in a Corinthian context in which people fight for hegemony (for controlling others, bodies of others). Kim, *Christ's Body in Corinth,* 65–95.

14. Indeed, there are a variety of related expressions about the meaning of Jesus' death. In Paul's undisputed letters there are implicit phrases about such a possibility: "died for us (1 Thess 5:10; Rom 5:8), "died for the ungodly" (Rom 5:6), "died for our sins" (1 Cor 15:3), "died for all" (2 Cor 5:14–15), and "died for nothing" (Gal 2:21). In the Gospels there are explicit connections between them: "poured out for many for the forgiveness of sins" (Matt 26:28) and "that repentance and forgiveness of sins is to be proclaimed" (Luke 24:47). In Acts there are a few similar phrases like Luke: Acts 5:31; 10:43; 13:38; 26:18. In Deutero-Pauline letters as well, there are clear expressions about them: "forgiveness of sins" (Col 1:14), "through the blood of his cross" (Col 1:20), "redemption through his blood, the forgiveness of our trespasses" (Eph 1:7), and "by the blood of Christ" (Eph 2:13). In 1 Peter are "sprinkled with his blood" (1 Pet 1:2), "with the precious blood of Christ" (1 Pet 1:19), and "suffered for sins once and for all" (1 Pet 3:18). Most notably, Hebrews is infused with the image of Jesus as the high priest who offers himself as atoning sacrifice with his blood (for example: Heb 2:17; 9:14). As a high priest, Jesus is "holy, blameless, undefiled, separated from sinners" (Heb 7:26). High priest appears fifteen times in Hebrew: Heb 2:17; 3:1; 4:14f; 5:1, 5, 10; 6:20; 7:26; 8:1, 3; 9:7, 11, 25; 13:11.

Markan community because it calls for an other-centered life. Jesus' death is a moral sacrifice for the dispossessed and the unfortunate. Jesus gives his life as ransom for many because they need justice in an unjust world (Mark 10:45). "Giving his life as ransom" is Jesus' faith for God and the world. In Mark, there is no need for Jesus' death for the forgiveness of sins. Rather, Jesus asks for repentance in his preaching early on in the narrative.

In Matthew, although there is a specific phrase "poured out for many for the forgiveness of sins" (Matt 26:28), this does not support the traditional atonement theory such as penal substitution. Unlike Hebrews, Matthew has only "the forgiveness of sins" without making a connection to "blood," as is the case with Deutero-Pauline letters and Hebrews, where the blood of Jesus has a role of cleansing sins (Eph 1:7; 2:13; 1 Pet 1:2, 19; Heb 2:17; 9:14). The primary sins in Matthew have to do with people's hypocrisy. Jesus is born to save people "from their sins" (Matt 1:21)—sins of arrogance and blindness to God's righteousness. Jesus as the Son of God will show and teach about God's rule so that people may change their hearts and seek God's rule or God's righteousness (Matt 6:33). Their sins in Matthew have to do with all kinds of thought or actions that do not seek God's rule. In this context of sins, Jesus' death then is understood as "the culmination of a life of integrity, a life that totally rejects every vestige of hypocrisy, even if this behavior leads to condemnation and death."[15] In Matthew, there is no explicit link between Jesus' death and the forgiveness of sins, as Jesus teaches how to pray: "Forgive us as we forgive others" (Matt 6:9–13).

In Luke, there is also "that repentance and forgiveness of sins is to be proclaimed" (Luke 24:47). Again, the questions are what kind of sins are involved or what does it mean that people are forgiven? In Luke, sins mainly have to do with people's ignorance about the Messiah and their wrongful killing of the Messiah. They repent for their ignorance and accept the Messiah as God's son for salvation. Jesus' death brings an opportunity for repentance because they wrongly killed the Messiah. The reason for repentance is their ignorance about the Messiah. Jesus' death in a historical context involves political charges against the Roman Empire, because he proclaimed the kingdom of God, not the kingdom of Rome.

John's Gospel does not contain a phrase such as "the forgiveness of sins," but does have a similar phrase that refers to Jesus as "the Lamb of God": "Here is the Lamb of God who takes away the sin of the world!" (John 1:29). Sin in John's gospel is not knowing God but rather dwelling in

15. Kim, "Jesus' Death in Context."

darkness, living a life apart from God. Put differently, sin is not to believe that Jesus is the Messiah who showed the works of God. In fact, in John's Gospel, sin is "singular and emphasizes the world's collective alienation from God and one another, rather than a catalog of human sin."[16]

In Paul's undisputed letters, Paul does not use the phrase "for the forgiveness of sins" and instead uses the phrase "died for." For example: "For while we were still weak, at the right time Christ died for the ungodly" (Rom 5:6); "But God proves his love for us in that while we still were sinners Christ died for us" (Rom 5:8); "Christ died for our sins" (1 Cor 15:3); "the love of Christ urges us on, . . . one has died for all; therefore all have died" (2 Cor 5:14); "And he died for all, so that those who live might live no longer for themselves, but for him who died and was raised for them" (2 Cor 5:15); "I do not nullify the grace of God; for if justification comes through the law, then Christ died for nothing" (Gal 2:21); "who died for us, so that whether we are awake or asleep we may live with him" (1 Thess 5:10). From the outset, Paul does not think of Jesus' death in terms of a sin offering (for example, a vicarious death to cleanse the sins of people) as opposed to other letters such as Deutero-Pauline letters and Hebrews where the blood of Jesus plays the role of purification of sinners (Eph 1:7; 2:13; 1 Pet 1:2, 19; Heb 2:17; 9:14). Christ died for people because they did not die. Christ showed moral examples and challenged people who were seeking their own lives at the expense of others. So "dying for people" is a moral sacrifice. Like Christ, people also have to die. Second Corinthians 5:14–15 makes clear that because Christ died for all, they all have died. Likewise, "Christ died for our sins" (1 Cor 15:3) can be understood as a moral sacrifice.

In Romans as well, the language of "Christ died for people" is Christ's faith example by which people have to follow his footsteps so that God's love may be proven (Rom 5:8) and that they may live not for themselves but for God and others (2 Cor 5:15). Even Gal 2:21 ("I do not nullify the grace of God; for if justification comes through the law, then Christ died for nothing") can be understood with this line of thought that Christ's death is confirmation of the grace of God; Christ exemplified God's grace through his life and death. Otherwise, right standing before God (justification) is not coming through any other way, including the law. God's grace comes first even before the law (see Romans 6–8). Unlike Luther's understanding of Paul, Paul does not mean the impossibility of the law *per se* as if the law

16. O'Day, "John," 1909.

were replaced by faith in Christ. Paul does not put the law against faith, or vice versa. Evidence in Romans is clear as he affirms the validity of the law and the place of Israel within God's covenant and promise. So the point is Jesus' death is a result of his faith.

Now some will ask, "What about the specific images about Jesus' death in Rom 3:25 where Jesus is put forward as *hilasterion* (the mercy seat or atonement)?" *Hilasterion* is the Greek translation of the Hebrew *kapporeh*, which means covering or the cover of the ark (mercy seat) used on the Day of Atonement, *Yom Kippur* (Exod 25:10–22; 37:1–9). In Hellenistic culture *hilasterion* means a propitiation, which has to do with appeasing an angry god. But this concept of appeasing god seems unfit to be applied here. Then, is Jesus' death like that of sacrificial victims whose blood is sprinkled on the cover of the ark so that the sins of people are covered? This option is plausible but not the best because Paul, overall, does not relate Jesus' death as a sin offering in his undisputed letters. Or, is *hilasterion* an expiation that something damaged has been mended? This is also plausible but not the best because Paul, overall, emphasizes Christian participation in Christ's death. Or, does Paul mean a mercy seat—God's presence on the cross of Jesus because of Christ's faith? This option is the best because it coheres with Paul's theology that Jesus' death is a result of his faithfulness to God's justice and love. Moreover, Jesus' faith is the condition that God begins a new era ruled by justice and love. Because of Jesus' faith, God declares that all previously committed sins have been dealt with now. But now is God's new time in which people have to respond to Jesus' death; that is the language of Christian participation or imitation of Christ.

Otherwise, Jesus' death in Paul's undisputed letters did not defeat evil once and for all and Jesus' followers are not completely out of the power of sin. Likewise, freedom is not gained for Jesus' followers once and for all because of Jesus' death. In Romans 7–8, Paul makes clear that the power of sin can be undone only when people put to death the deeds of the body (Rom 8:13–14): "For if you live according to the flesh, you will die; but if by the Spirit you put to death the deeds of the body, you will live. For all who are led by the Spirit of God are children of God." In Rom 7:4, Paul says, "you have died to the law through the body of Christ, so that you may belong to another, to him who has been raised from the dead in order that we may bear fruit for God." "Dying to the law" means dying to the law of sin, and "through the body of Christ" means "through Christ's body"—a way of Christ's life imagined with his crucifixion. Taken together, the whole verse can be put like this: "You have died to the law of sin that seeks your fleshly desires through the example of Christ's body—an image of his crucifixion that speaks about his obedience to the will of God. By dying like Christ, you belong to Christ and bear fruit for God." In this regard, Wright's view of Jesus' death is awry, as he put it: "Jesus' death did accomplish the real defeat of the evil that had infected Israel along with the rest of the world."[17] Evil or sin is not defeated once and for all. It can become powerless only when Jesus' followers "put to death the deeds of the body" (Rom 8:13). That is what Paul calls their "baptism into his death" (Rom 6:4). In order to live to God, they have to die with him, which means they have to control their bodily deeds. It is Paul's conviction that without their participation in Jesus' death, there would be neither life to God nor freedom in Christ. In other words, Jesus' death itself does not make people free without their participation in his death.

In sum, Jesus' death is understood in his love of God and the world. Jesus was faithful to God in disclosing God's righteousness in a dangerous world where people desperately need God's rule. Jesus' faith is an example of his love of God, and at the same time, it is an expression of his love of the world—a masterpiece of God's creation. Jesus' death is also a judgment for the world—a symbol of evil powers and rulers. Those who are accountable for his death are judged through God's vindication of Jesus.

But as time goes by, later epistles highlight the blood of Jesus for the forgiveness of sins without paying attention to the historical reason of Jesus' death (Eph 1:7; 2:13; 1 Pet 1:2, 19; Heb 2:17; 9:14). Most notably, Hebrews refers to Jesus' death as the perfect sacrifice that replaces the animal sacrifice of the old covenant (Heb 7:26). In it, Jesus himself is the High Priest, who becomes a new covenant; we see here some kind of supercessionism in which a new covenant replaces the old covenant, which is out of context if we read "a new covenant" in Jer 31:31–34 in a historical, literary context, because a new covenant in Jeremiah is made with the house of Israel and the house of Judah, and would not apply for later Christians.

SUMMARY

While the later epistles (Hebrews, Deutero-Pauline letters, 1 Peter) emphasize the meaning of Jesus' death with a focus on the forgiveness of sins and a perfect one-time sacrifice of a sin offering, Paul's undisputed letters and the

17. Wright, *Mission and Message of Jesus*, 51.

canonical Gospels present Jesus' death as a result of his bold preaching of God's good news that God, not the Roman emperor or any ideologies, must rule in an unjust world. As Mark 10:45 reads, his death has to do with serving the marginalized. Jesus in Mark is the suffering Son of God who walks the walk of suffering for those who need God's rule and justice. In Luke, Jesus dies as a martyr or prophet, as he hints early on in his ministry (Luke 4:16–30). Even in John's Gospel Jesus' death is a result of his testimony to the truth of God. The reason that he is led to the cross is not very different from what is told in the Synoptic Gospels. He dies because of his faith and love of God and the world. As I wrote elsewhere, "Jesus made the ultimate sacrifice because of a love that drove him to question and even to defy the accepted customs (context) of life in his society. In doing so, he incited the hatred of religious and political authorities of his time."[18] It is Jesus' choices that "created a moral loneliness that put him outside the context of his society and on the cross, a loneliness voiced in the cry, 'My God, my God, why have you forsaken me.'"[19]

18. Kim, "Jesus' Death in Context."
19. Ibid.

6

The Resurrection of Jesus

How CAN WE UNDERSTAND the resurrection of Jesus from historical and theological perspectives? Where can we put the resurrection narrative in the larger cultural context of the Greco-Roman and Jewish worlds? What does the language of resurrection have to do with Jesus' death and his followers? While some believe that the resurrection of Jesus is literal and a bodily one in the sense that Jesus has a new body, others bluntly reject the bodily resurrection. Still others hold a moderate view that resurrection is not provable or refutable because it is beyond human faculty. In the following, I will briefly state the interpretation history about the resurrection of Jesus before we examine the resurrection accounts in the New Testament and their meaning.

REVIEW OF INTERPRETATION

The Literal, Bodily Resurrection

The view of a literal, bodily resurrection represents a traditional Christian confession like the Apostle's Creed.[1] Every Sunday, many Christians recite their belief in the bodily resurrection, which in a way rejects death, whether physical or spiritual. Bodily resurrection affirms the continuity of this (bodily) life in the future when the Lord returns at the Parousia.

1. Borg and Wright, *Meaning of Jesus,* 111–27.

But this view is not supported by some scriptures. The risen Jesus is not recognized by the two disciples when he walks with them on the road to Emmaus (Luke 24:13–35); this means he is not the same as he used to be. Jesus seems a mystery and he is only recognized when he eats with them. Perhaps what this story conveys is that Jesus cannot be recognized with bodily or physical looks but through spiritual relationships. Another similar episode about Jesus' resurrection appearance comes from John, where Mary Magdalene cannot recognize the risen Lord in a tomb. She thought of Jesus as a guard of the tomb, but when Jesus calls her "Mary" she knew that he was Jesus. Again, this story also conveys the idea that the risen Jesus is recognized not by his physical looks but by remembering what he did or said when he was alive.

Of course, there are other scriptures that confirm Jesus' bodily resurrection as he shows the marks of nails to his disciples (John 20:20). But it is very plausible that these kinds of bodily resurrection accounts are from post-Easter experience that cannot be taken as accurately historical.

Paul's testimony is significant in this regard. He affirms the resurrection of the dead (1 Cor 15:12), which is different from the bodily resurrection. The former does not require the body and the emphasis is God's power or victory against the power of evil. In addition, Paul says "flesh and blood cannot inherit the kingdom of God" (1 Cor 15:50). Paul says there is a completely different reality/world at the resurrection, which is unlike the bodily human world. When Paul refers to Jesus' resurrection, he always emphasizes that it is God who raised Jesus (for example, Rom 1:3; 6:4), which is a language of theology that underscores God's power against the power of evil or death. According to Paul, those who hold the view of a literal, bodily resurrection may be compared to Corinthians who asked Paul: "How are the dead raised? With what kind of body do they come?" (15:35).

The Empty Tomb

While some take the empty tomb story in the Gospels as proof of Jesus' resurrection, others reject that idea. H. S. Reimarus (1694–1768) thinks that the charge that the disciples of Jesus stole the body of Jesus (Matt 28:11–15) is correct. In a different note, H. E. G. Paulus (1761–1861) believes that Jesus seemed to have died and then returned to life.[2] Still others such as

2. Paulus, *Kommentar über die drey ersten Evangelien*, 797–806, 839–931; *Das Leben Jesu*, 277–305.

H. J. Holtzmann (1832–1910) and J. Klausner explain that the empty tomb existed because Joseph of Arimathea reburied the body of Jesus, moving it from a temporary place to a permanent one.[3] Quite interestingly, however, according to Daniel Smith, the empty tomb story in Mark that does not include Jesus' resurrection story can be evidence of assumption (the taking up of the righteous).[4] That is, the idea here is that Jesus was taken up to heaven by God like Elijah or Enoch. The sense of assumption may be indicated in the so-called Q gospel 13:35 (Luke 13:35) where Jesus says: "You will not see me until the time comes." This means that Jesus comes back as the Lord since he was taken up by God.

But Paul is silent about the empty tomb in his letters; rather he points out the importance of God's power and Jesus' exaltation in Phil 2:9 where there is no reference to the empty tomb. Therefore, it is very plausible that the story of the empty tomb is a product of the early church that aims at maintaining its faith in a difficult hostile world.[5]

The Subjective Vision Theory

The subjective vision theory says that the disciples of Jesus met Jesus in their visions. It argues that the resurrection is not a hallucination but a subjective vision real to his disciples. Proponents of this view include D. F. Strauss and C. Holsten (1825–1897), who argue that Jesus' disciples had to resolve the psychological conflict between the once living Messiah and the dead one now, and came to realize that they saw the risen Jesus with their enthusiasm about their ongoing faith.[6] Similarly, G. Lüdemann also argues for the subjective vision theory that Peter's and Paul's vision of Jesus take center stage in proclamation about Jesus.[7]

---

3. Holtzmann, "Das leere Grab," 79–86, 119–32; Klausner, *Jesus of Nazareth*, 357.

4. Kloppenborg, *Q the Earliest Gospel*, 84. For assumption theology, see also Smith, "Revisiting the Empty Tomb," 123–37. See also Zeller, "Entrückung zur Ankunft als Menschensohn (Luke 13:34f.; 11:29f.)," 513–30.

5. Stanton, *Gospels and Jesus*, 290.

6. Strauss, *Life of Jesus Critically Examined*, 350–74. See also Holsten, "Die Christus-Vision."

7. Lüdemann, *Resurrection of Christ*, 47–49.

Post-Easter Christian Kerygma

This view reflects some recent historical critical scholarship in that the historical Jesus is distinguished from Christ proclaimed and confessed by his followers and the early church after his death.[8] In other words, Easter is understood as Jesus' followers' faith rather than as a historical event. That is, the historical Jesus is remembered and reinterpreted as the suffering Messiah and the Son of Man who will come back to bring an end to the current chaotic world. As such, Rudolf Bultmann and W. Wrede make a distinction between the historical Jesus and Christ of faith and argue that new faith begins with the early Christian *kerygma*, which is not based on the historical Jesus.[9] In this view, resurrection accounts in the synoptic tradition reflect the post-Easter faith.[10]

Resurrection as a Metaphor

Among others, J. D. Crossan interprets the resurrection of Jesus metaphorically as God's victory over evil.[11] It is the disciples' faith that Jesus is alive and raised by God. Resurrection is a sign that God intervenes in human history and turns upside down the status quo of human society and evil. Jesus' crucifixion may have been the end of the story, but that is not the end. Jesus' resurrection is assurance that those who struggle with injustice in the world have a hope for victory in the end. In this regard, the early Christians interpreted Jesus' death through the eye of God's victory and God's resurrection of Jesus. It is their faith in God's victory and therefore Jesus' triumph not because of his death but because of his work of justice.

---

8. For example, M. Borg and J. D. Crossan.

9. Wrede, *Messianic Secret in the Gospels*. See also Bultmann, "Die Frage nach dem messianischen," 165–74.

10. Marxsen, *Resurrection of Jesus*, 31. For Marxsen, Easter means proclaiming the message of the earthly Jesus and an ongoing experience of the risen Jesus in the community. Bultmann's existentialist interpretation, Karl Barth's revelation interpretation, and W. Pannenberg's universal history interpretation belong to this way of interpretation about the resurrection of Jesus. See Bultmann, "Auferstehungsgeschichten," 245; "Problem," 120–21. See Barth, *Church Dogmatic* IV, 1:304, 334; See Pannenberg, *Systematic Theology*, 2:343–63; *Jesus God and Man*, 53–114; *Basic Questions in Theology* I, 15–80; *Revelation in History*, 123–58.

11. Crossan, "Resurrection," 23–44.

RESURRECTION IN THE HEBREW BIBLE AND JEWISH TRADITION

The Hebrew Bible is mainly concerned with phenomenon of this world.[12] Life in this world is essential and must flourish on earth as God blesses the first human family: "be fruitful and multiply, and fill the earth" (Gen 1:28). Accordingly, justice and peace should be established in this world. Reward and punishment also occur in this world (Deut 11:16–17; 28:15–68). Death seems to be final in the Hebrew Bible except for Enoch and Elijah (Gen 5:21–24; 1 Kings 2:11).[13] At Moses' death, there is no mention of afterlife for him (Deut 34:5–8). The dead go to *sheol* (a deep pit), a kind of shadowy existence, with no form of life and with complete separation from the living world (Isa 5:14; 38:1–10, 18–19; Prov 27:20; Job 7:9–10; 10:10–21; 14:21–22; 17:13–16; Ps 30:9–10; 88:11–13; 139:8; Gen 37:35; 42:38).[14]

But gradually, the idea of resurrection came into being in the Hebrew Bible, though it is difficult to draw the line when exactly it happened.[15] A large line can be drawn from the second century BCE on the one hand, when Daniel was written in response to "Antiochus IV's reign and killing of the pious Jews,"[16] and on the other hand, a small line can also be drawn from the Hebrew Bible, namely, from the notion of God as an almighty, source of life, creator, redeemer, and sustainer. With this thought, bodily resurrection is not impossible with God. A prominent line can be drawn by the second century BCE, the beginning of a period of enormous suffering for the pious Jews.[17] Antiochus IV's cruel reign of Judea and his attempt to annihilate the Jewish religion gave rise to Jewish protests. As a result, many righteous Jews were killed and persecuted. Daniel was written in response to this situation of unjustified evil and the suffering of the righteous.[18] Daniel 12:1–3 affirms God's vindication for those who died unjustly and

---

12. Knight, "Ethics and Human Life," 82.

13. Finality of death can be found in Ps 6:6; 30:9–10; 39:13–14; 49:6–13; 146:2–4; 115:16–18; Isa 38:18–19; Job 10:20–22; 14:1–10.

14. Gillman, *Death of Death*, 65–68.

15. Isa 25:7–8 and 26:18–19 seem to connote the idea of resurrection but they should be understood in the exilic context where people need hope for a restored Israel. In the same vein, Ezek 37:11–12 is not a reference to the notion of bodily resurrection but it should be taken as a metaphor for the restoration of Israel.

16. Gillman, *Death of Death*, 86–87.

17. Ibid.

18. Collins, *Commentary on the Book of Daniel*, 392.

His punishment for those who are evil: "Many of those that sleep in the dust of the earth will awake, some to eternal life, others to reproaches, to everlasting abhorrence. And the knowledgeable will be radiant like the bright expanse of sky, and those who lead the many to righteousness will be like the stars forever."

Daniel's affirmation of God's vindication is clearly understandable in light of the theodicy that God will certainly reward those righteous persons, and that God will punish those who are evil.[19] The question is, why is the second century BCE a starting point rather than other historically difficult times in biblical history, for example, the time of exile in Babylonia (586 BCE). The answer is this: the Babylonian exile was interpreted as a result of Israel's sin.[20] So in this case, God's justice was not questioned. This interpretation was of the Deuteronomic School, which emphasized the system of reward and punishment. But the situation of the second century BCE was different because of the massive unjust suffering of the Israelites caused by Antiochus IV. The pious Jews then questioned God's justice and came up with the idea of God's justice in the future through bodily resurrection. Here bodily resurrection became the means of God's justice (vindication) for the righteous. The pious Jews had the conviction that God would take care of them even beyond this earthly life because "God is omnipotent, compassionate and just."[21] Does that conviction include heaven as a place for the righteous? This is a difficult question to answer, but the possibility of heaven is not completely ruled out in the apocalyptic context where the righteous people need an immediate solution and comfort in the midst of suffering. Daniel 12:2–3 expresses with apocalyptic language the urgent need for God's vindication, through which everlasting life will be given. In this sense, this "everlasting life" (12:2) could be interpreted as a sort of immortality of the soul. But that is not the end. The idea of everlasting life involves bodily resurrection, though the notion of bodily resurrection is not yet fully developed. For example, Daniel 12:1–3 is not concerned with "the resurrection of masses of Jews, nor with the resurrection of all the dead, nor the dead of prior generations."[22] Later in rabbinic Judaism, the idea of afterlife was developed with emphasis on both elements of the everlasting life: bodily resurrection and immortality of the soul.

19. Stewart, *Rabbinic Theology*, 142.
20. Gillman, *Death of Death*, 86.
21. Ibid., 88.
22. Ibid., 88–89.

Extra-biblical parallels of the second century BCE to the second century CE should also be included in the discussion of bodily resurrection. These parallels can be understood as Daniel in the context of God's justice for the righteous and his punishment of evil. See the following quotes from various extra-biblical materials.

> The righteous one shall arise from his sleep. (Enoch 91:10)

> The righteous one shall awaken from his sleep; he shall arise and walk in the ways of righteousness. . . (Enoch 92:2)

> You, you fiend are making us depart from present life, but the King of the universe will resurrect us, who die for the sake of His laws, to a new eternal life. (2 Macc 7:9)

> Surely, then, the creator of the universe, who shaped man's coming into being . . . with mercy will restore spirit and life to you. . . (2 Macc 7:22–23)

> The earth shall give up those who are asleep in it, and the dust those who dwell silently in it. (4 Ezra 7:32)

> God himself will again form the bones and ashes of men, and he will raise up mortals again, as they were before. And then judgment will take place. (Sibyline Oracle IV:180)

> Then you will see Enoch, Noah and Shem, and Abraham, Isaac, and Jacob rising on the right hand in gladness. Then we also shall rise, each over our tribe, . . .then all will rise, some to glory and some to dishonor. (Testament of Benjamin 10:6–8)

Enoch 91:10 spells out the necessity of arising from sleep because the righteous persons should be vindicated. The idea of resurrection is similarly expressed here as in Dan 12:2. Overall, the above parallels both extend and expand the earlier notion of bodily resurrection found in Daniel. They are extensions in terms of God's vindication of justice, but more than that, they are expansions: "God is more powerful than death."[23] Second Maccabees 7:9 and 7:22–23 indicate that God is more than justice; now God gives a new eternal life because God is merciful and is creator of the universe. Another interesting development of the notion of bodily resurrection comes from the Testament of Benjamin 10:6–8, where ancestors of the Jews are also included in the resurrection.

23. Ibid., 105.

THE IMMORTALITY OF THE SOUL

It is important to distinguish between the resurrection in the New Testament and the immortality of the soul. The immortality of the soul is no doubt a Greek thought as rooted in Socrates or Plato. For example, in Plato's dialogue, *Phaedo*, Socrates views death as good because the soul can be liberated from the body at death.[24] In the Hebrew Bible, there is no concept of a dualistic body as in Greek philosophy. In Greek thought, a human is composed of a body and a soul. The soul is immortal but the body perishes. So death is necessary and good; otherwise, the soul cannot attain immortality. But the Hebrew Bible in general does not support the notion of immortality of the soul. The Bible portrays death as final even though there are good deaths: Abraham, Isaac, Jacob, and Moses, for example. All of these people died in their old age and were gathered to their ancestors.

Genesis 2:7 and Ecclesiastes 12:7 are often quoted as biblical references to the immortality of the soul. "The Lord God formed *Adam* from the soil of the ground (*adamah*) and breathed into his nostrils *the breath of life*, and Adam became *a living being*" (Gen 2:7). "And the dust returns to the earth as it was, and the spirit returns to God who gave it" (Eccl 12:7). The breath of life (Gen 2:7) is *nishmat* in Hebrew, meaning "breath" which animates a human being into a living being (*nefesh*). The word *nefesh* means a whole person, life force, but it is not the soul in the Greek concept.[25] While in the original context *nefesh* is a single entity, which cannot be separated between body and soul, in the rabbinic tradition this term came to be understood as soul. Ecclesiastes 12:7 does not support the dichotomy of a human being as composed of a body and a soul. It is actually an extension of Gen 2:7 in the sense that the spirit as God's animating breath returns to God, which is not the same as the soul of Greek.[26] From the Bible there is hardly a notion of a soul that survives death. Then, from where does this idea of immortality of the soul come? The general scholarly agreement situates it in Greek thought and philosophy where human life is viewed dualistically: body and soul. This borrowed idea of the immortality of the soul appears in the Wisdom of Solomon:

> And they did not know the secret purposes of God, nor hope for
> the wages of holiness, nor discern the prize for *blameless souls*; for

24. Gillman, *Death of Death*, 75.

25. Bailey, *Biblical Perspectives on Death*, 42.

26. Ibid.

> God created man for *incorruption*, and made him in the image of his own *eternity*, but through the devil's envy death entered the world, and those who belong to his party experience it. (Wisdom of Solomon 2:22–24)

> But the *souls* of the righteous are in the hand of God, and no torment will ever touch them. In the eyes of the foolish they seemed to have died, and their departure was thought to be an affliction, and their going from us to be their destruction; but they are at peace. For though in the sight of men they were punished, their hope is full of *immortality*. (Wisdom of Solomon 3:1–4)

As seen from the above, the language of "blameless souls" and "incorruption" is closely related with the Greek idea of immortality of the soul (2:22–24). In 3:1–4, the immortality of the soul is the theme.

JESUS' VIEW OF RESURRECTION

According to Josephus, the Pharisees believe in an afterlife: "Their belief is that souls have a deathless vigor, and that beneath the earth there are rewards and punishments according as they have been devoted in life to virtue or vice . . . but the former shall have *the power to revive and live again*" (*Antiquities of the Jews* 18: I:3). In contrast, the Sadducees deny resurrection altogether. It should be noted that the Pharisees take a middle position that seems to combine elements of the bodily resurrection and the immortality of the soul.

Jesus also believes in resurrection, but his view of resurrection is different from the Pharisees' because he denies the bodily nature of the future resurrection as recorded in Mark 12:18–27; Matt 22:23–33; Luke 20:27–40. He answers the Sadducees' question "In the resurrection, then, whose wife of the seven will she be? For all of them had married her" (Matt 22:28): "You are wrong, because you know neither the scriptures nor the power of God. For in the resurrection they neither marry nor are given in marriage, but are like angels in heaven. And as for the resurrection of the dead, have you not read what was said to you by God, 'I am the God of Abraham, the God of Isaac, and the God of Jacob'? He is God not of the dead, but of the living" (Matt 22:29–32).

While affirming a general resurrection on the last day, Jesus thinks of the angelic status of the resurrection. But what Jesus really wants to emphasize in his answer is that resurrection is not a matter of the past or the future but a matter of the present. God is with people now: "He is God not of the dead, but of the living" (Matt 22:32). In John's Gospel too, Jesus answers Martha who understands the resurrection only as the future event: "I am the resurrection and the life. Those who believe in me, even though they die, will live" (John 11:25).

EARLY CHRISTIAN UNDERSTANDING ABOUT RESURRECTION

Early Christian understanding of the resurrection of Jesus should not be taken as "literal" in ways that Jesus' physical body returns. Resurrection in the New Testament is faith language, not science or a provable fact. That faith must be understood properly within the historical context of early Christian communities. On the one hand, early Christians, after Jesus' death, could not accept that Jesus failed by dying on a cross. This question by early Christians needs an answer from God, which is we call the vindication of Jesus. God's vindication of Jesus is the resurrection of him as we read in narrative gospels such as Matthew or Luke. But according to a hypothetical gospel Q, which is sayings gospel that began in Galilee and is claimed as the earliest gospel, God's vindication may be understood differently; that is through the notion of *assumption* (taking up of the righteous).[27] As John S. Kloppenborg shows in his work, Jesus may have meant such a view of assumption as indicated in Q 13:35 (Luke 13:35), which "recalls Elijah's or Enoch's departure": "See, your house is left to you. And I tell you, you will not see me until the time comes when you say, 'Blessed is the one who comes in the name of the Lord.'"[28]

In either case of the vindication, the point is that Jesus is vindicated by the almighty God. Their faith is that Jesus did not fail on a cross; he died "the death of a just man or a prophet whom God had 'taken up'" according to the assumption theory. And according to Matthew or Luke, God's vindication is fully narrated in connection with the bodily resurrection of Jesus. So much so the four Evangelists (Matthew, Luke, Mark, and John), believing that Jesus is with them spiritually, respectively reinterpret Jesus' work and death in view of God's salvific plan for the world.

27. Kloppenborg, *Q the Earliest Gospel*, 84; Smith, "Revisiting the Empty Tomb," 123–37; Smith, *Post-Mortem Vindication of Jesus*.

28. Kloppenborg, *Q the Earliest Gospel*, 84.

But even with this notion of bodily resurrection in the canonical narrative gospels, the caveat is this: the resurrection of Jesus in the New Testament cannot be fully understood if we are stuck with the *bodily* resurrection in the sense that he returned with his earthly physical look. Then some will ask, "How should we understand Jesus' entering the room without opening the door or about his walking with two disciples on the road to Emmaus without being recognized by them (Luke 24:13–35)?" But I ask again: "Did Jesus' face change? Or, is this story only of a spiritual dimension that tells us of the importance of the risen Jesus' spiritual power or presence in our lives?" If we read these appearance accounts as moral or spiritual stories, they are understood well. In this way of thinking about the resurrection in the Gospels, even if Jesus' bones were found, it will not reduce the importance of the resurrection story focused on God's power to vindicate Jesus. Probably, the early followers of Jesus must have known the full story regarding the tomb of Jesus. Perhaps, they must have known that the bones of Jesus were collected and deposited in a box, maybe in Talpiot discovered in 1980.

Some will still ask, "Is the empty tomb evidence of Jesus' bodily resurrection?" Well, logically speaking, the empty tomb itself cannot be the evidence of the bodily resurrection because, for example, somebody can spread the rumor that Jesus' body was stolen, as we hear in Matt 28:13: "His disciples came by night and stole him away while we were asleep." Or in some other situation it is possible that the tomb of Joseph of Arimathea is only for a temporary burial (Jewish custom for the time of being rotten) and that the corpse of Jesus was moved to the other permanent burial place with bone boxes.

Given the above, perhaps early Christian witnesses refer to some form of a spiritual resurrection. Even Paul says that Jesus became a "life-giving spirit" (1 Cor 15:45). All in all, the whole point is that Jesus did not fail because of the cross. According to Q, Jesus died as a prophet, which is necessary. In the following, we will see in detail how each Evangelist and Paul's letters talk about the resurrection of Jesus.

Resurrection in the Gospels

All the Gospels are from forty to sixty years after Jesus' death. Supposedly, the very early story about Jesus may not involve a passion narrative or resurrection narrative at all, as the hypothetical gospel Q contains only Jesus' sayings or teaching material without narratives about birth, passion, or resurrection. Of course, this does not mean that early followers of Jesus made up such narratives out of context. Resurrection, as seen before, is supposed to be Jesus' followers' logical response to Jesus' death, which is reflected in the Gospels. However, the resurrection in the Gospels cannot be taken literally; it must be seen as a theological language of faith that speaks about God's vindication of Jesus because of Jesus' faithful work.

In Mark, the earliest written Gospel among the canonical Gospels, there is no resurrection appearance of the risen Lord according to the shorter ending at 16:8. The longer ending up to 16:20 is believed to be later editors' insertion to make this gospel look like Matthew. In the shorter ending, there are no angels or the risen Lord appearing directly, eating with his disciples such as in Luke or John. Instead, women who visit the tomb of Jesus (Mary Magdalene, and Mary the mother of James, and Salome) hear the news of the risen Lord from a young man and are told to tell this news to other male disciples so that they come to Galilee to meet Jesus. The point of this story is not that the tomb is empty; the young man tells of the good news about the resurrection, and the gospel ends with women fearing about this good news.

That ending may seem ironic because they presumably should be joyful at that good news; instead, they are dumbfounded. The text does not explicitly state what it is that they fear. The readers/hearers of this gospel can react or respond to such a weird ending by raising a question: "If I were one of these women, what would be my response?" They perhaps represent the context of the Markan community which faces persecution and hardships because of their new faith in God through Jesus. It is like a choice of life or death for members of the Markan community. If faith is chosen, they may be risking their lives. In the passion narrative of Mark, Jesus walks the thorny path that he wished to avoid. But he chooses not what he wants, but what God wants. That is what the faith journey means in Mark.

In Matthew, we see a fully developed story about Jesus including his birth, teaching, passion, and resurrection. The resurrection narrative in Matthew shows a few distinctive features compared with Mark. First, there are supernatural or miraculous deeds of God: an earthquake, an angel of the Lord descending from heaven, his appearance is like lightning, and his clothing white as snow. Second, women leave the tomb with fear and great joy after they hear about Jesus from the angel. Women are trusted and seen as great disciples who tell this good news to the other disciples. Because of these women's testimony, male disciples gather around Jesus.[29] Third, when they leave, Jesus meets these women on the way and speaks to them: "Do not be afraid; go and tell my brothers to go to Galilee; there they will see me" (Matt 28:10). Fourth, there is a motif about the empty tomb. Jerusalem leaders worry about Jesus' body because some may attempt to steal it and claim that Jesus has risen. Fifth, Jesus commissions the disciples on the mountain in Galilee and sends them out to all the people. Lastly, Jesus promises to be with them until the end of the age.

The resurrection episode in Luke is similar to, yet different from, Matthew. Like Matthew, the basic description about the resurrection is similar: the stone rolled away from the tomb, messengers (two men) appearing, and women commissioned to tell the news to other disciples. But it also differs from Matthew because the risen Lord does not appear to women visitors. The implication is that the risen Lord cannot be easily recognized by his physical looks; that is why Luke adds another episode about the resurrection, a story about two disciples meeting Jesus on the way to Emmaus. This seemingly strange story is being told to support not so much Jesus' bodily (physical) resurrection but to affirm the resurrection of Jesus according to the scriptures (or by God). Two disciples walk with a stranger but they do not recognize that he is Jesus. This means that the risen Jesus does not look the same as before. But the real problem is not Jesus' different appearance but their ignorance or oblivion to Jesus' ministry and death. Two disciples tell Jesus about what happened in Jerusalem. They say they believed Jesus was going to redeem Israel, but instead he was condemned to death by leaders. Though some women say they heard about Jesus' resurrection through angels, they still cannot believe it. When Jesus breaks the bread with them, they confess: "Were not our hearts burning within us while he was talking to us on the road, while he was opening the scriptures to us?" (24:32); this confession can be understood as their resurrection faith, not based on Jesus' physical resurrection but through their personal spiritual experience with him. Later, they return to Jerusalem and proclaim about Jesus' resurrection without having confirmed it with their eyes or by looking at his face: "The Lord has risen indeed, and he has appeared to Simon!" (24:34).

Here we have to point out the fact that only after this episode of Emmaus, the risen Lord appears to his disciples gathered in Jerusalem, finally showing his flesh and bones. This hints that Luke thinks from solution to

29. Wainwright, *Shall We Look for Another*, 114.

the plight; the solution says Jesus was resurrected; the plight is difficulties about Jesus' resurrection. Even the solution is not based in Jesus' personal appearance; there is no direct encounter between Jesus and his disciples unlikely in Matthew. Rather, the solution is based on their faith and interpretation of the scriptures related to Jesus. Based on this conviction about Jesus' resurrection, they solve difficulties in understanding his resurrection. This is where the risen Lord personally appears to them. Otherwise, this appearance of the risen Lord should not be read to emphasize the bodily nature of his resurrection, because even when Jesus greets them with "peace be with you" the gathered disciples "were startled and terrified, and thought that they were seeing a ghost" (24:37). This resurrection scene serves to strengthen their belief in the resurrection: "Why are you frightened, and why do doubts arise in your hearts?" (24:38).

John's resurrection narrative is certainly different from Matthew's or Luke's. But the basic understanding of the resurrection of Jesus is close to Luke's. First, both of them have extended stories about the resurrection. In the case of John, there is the risen Lord's appearing at the sea of the Tiberias and eating with his disciples. Second, as in Luke, the risen Lord is not recognized by his disciples, which implies that the encounter with the risen Lord is not with the eyes but through the presence of the spirit of Jesus. Jesus says to them, "Come and have breakfast" (21:12). "Now none of the disciples dared to ask him, 'Who are you?' because they knew it was the Lord" (21:12). Jesus "took the bread and gave it to them, and did the same with the fish" (21:13). At this very moment, his disciples suddenly recognize the risen Lord. Nobody asks, "Who are you?" because they see, feel, touch, and experience the risen Lord.

This farewell meal prepared by the risen Lord serves as a symbolic moment of renewal for the Johannine community, which affirms and continues the ministry of Jesus. Remembering his work, the community now sees, eats, touches, and feels the very presence of Jesus the spirit. Before his return to the Father, Jesus appears three times to make sure that they continue his teachings. In fact, the narrator says this is the third time Jesus appears to the disciples. After this communal meal together, Jesus asks Peter three times "do you love me?" Jesus' question to Peter is inviting and mends broken a relationship between him and Peter.

Resurrection in the Undisputed Letters of Paul

Paul also understands that the resurrection may be close to "a life-giving spirit" (1 Cor 15:45).[30] In Paul's mind, Jesus is the start of this new resurrection, and Jesus' followers will be transformed into this kind of spiritual existence in the future: "It is sown a physical body, it is raised a *spiritual body*. If there is a physical body, there is also a spiritual body" (1 Cor 15:44). A spiritual body is like saying a round triangle because in Greek philosophy, the body and the spirit cannot go together. While the body is rotten, the spirit lives forever. But Paul here affirms the resurrection wisely: the resurrection body is not physical or flesh but spiritual. If we think about a body at all, the body of resurrection is not the body that we know; it is a "spiritual body"—a kind of spiritual life we can imagine. Otherwise, it is simply unknowable. That is why Paul uses such a strange phrase like "spiritual body." Like Jesus, Paul does not think that the physical body is somehow maintained with the resurrection. Paul clearly rejects the flesh/body resurrection, as he says, "Flesh and blood cannot inherit the kingdom of God, nor does the perishable inherit the imperishable" (1 Cor 15:50). Paul knows that the body dies and is rotten. It is a physical body. The resurrection is God's business. The only thing Paul says or Jesus imagines is that God is in charge of all and everything. The resurrection is a new life, not physical but spiritual: it is a spiritual body that defies any standard definition.

When it comes to Deutero-Pauline or Pastoral letters, there is virtually no resurrection of Jesus mentioned except for 2 Tim 2:18, where the author warns those who claim that the resurrection has already taken place. The later churches become more adaptive to the social environment, on one hand, becoming very conservative in their view of community (e.g., gender relations and hierarchical offices in the church), and on the other hand, settled in the present life. There is no urgency of the Parousia (Col 1:13; Eph 1:4, 26; 2:12–13), and God's creation is good here; therefore, marriage and childbirth are encouraged (1 Tim 4:1–5). Even the end is not coming without signs (2 Thess 2:2–12). All of these are contrasted with Paul's views as we have seen before.

---

30. Interestingly, 1 Peter 3:18 also has a similar tone with Paul: "He was put to death in the flesh, but made alive in the spirit."

SUMMARY OF RESURRECTION

In this chapter we have explored the resurrection of Jesus from a variety of perspectives. We surveyed the seed of the resurrection idea from the Hebrew Bible, Second Temple Judaism, and in Jewish traditions in the first century. We also reflected on Jesus' view about the resurrection. All of these taken together, lead us to conclude this: the resurrection is not a unique concept or thing applied to Jesus. Rather, it is a faith language that was started long before Jesus.

We also examined the Gospels and Paul's letters. Here resurrection language is not a physical or bodily concept but a spiritual one, as is shown in Luke or John. Paul's testimony is more powerful than the Gospels. He says Jesus becomes a life-giving spirit. In 1 Corinthians, Paul denies the concept of a bodily resurrection if it is understood as having flesh and blood. In Hellenistic philosophy, and in Paul's time, the body is to the spirit what water is to oil. Therefore, in the end, Paul's point is this: there is the resurrection of the dead because it is God's power. But he cannot explicate it other than using an oxymoronic phrase such as a spiritual body. Below is a brief summary of the resurrection in the New Testament.

Resurrection as the Language of Faith

The resurrection in the New Testament must be understood as the language of faith that deals with present lives in crisis or danger. In other words, the bodily (flesh) resurrection is a distortion to the faith language, because natural death is not wrong in itself, and the flesh and the blood are given by God for blessings of human life. Denial of the body or flesh is not found in the New Testament. What is wrong with the body (flesh) is not that it is rotten but people live in the flesh with a crooked heart. Jesus' life shows his faith in God, so that even death did not swallow him completely. The message is that people have to live by a similar faith.

Resurrection as a Spiritual Body

The resurrection language in the Gospels and Paul's letters in particular must be understood as "a spiritual body" which is more than a metaphor; it points to a reality empowered by God. Once we try to explain, there is a lapse. As Jesus became a life-giving spirit, Jesus' followers will also become like that.

Resurrection as God's Victory

The resurrection in the New Testament must be understood as God's victory or God's business, and not as Jesus' business. Jesus finished the work given by God, as he says "it is finished" in John 19:30. The rest is not his job. In the Synoptic Gospels, Jesus is adopted as the Son of God at his baptism, and does his work; the rest is not his job. Similarly, Paul emphasizes the gospel of the cross rather than the resurrection of glory because the resurrection is God's business; there is nothing one can do about it. However, in taking up the cross of Jesus, people can have a tremendous influence and impact on the world.

Resurrection as Testimony and Transformation

Early Christians testified to Jesus' work by claiming God's vindication of Jesus, which is the resurrection faith. As Jesus did not give up on his thorny faith journey, Jesus' followers are encouraged to do the same, because the rest is God's business. The resurrection is a testimony to God's work done through Jesus and continues to be testified through his followers. Their fear is overcome while continuing to face dangers or difficulties because of their testimony in the world. By testifying to God's work done through Jesus, early Christians go through a process of transformation, rooted in God's love and hope. Jesus' disciples in Luke are reawakened to the ministry of Jesus when they meet Jesus through the eyes of faith. Jesus' disciples in John are also recovered to the core of Jesus' ministry only when they feel the presence of the risen Lord. In particular, the resurrection in John may be understood as perpetual in the sense that a new life (eternal life) begins in the here and now, and continues forever. Otherwise, there is no yearning for a remote future.

7

New Testament Theology and Today

WE HAVE COME FULL circle now. In the beginning I raised issues regarding New Testament theology and proposed an alternative approach to it by emphasizing the work of the historical Jesus. Then throughout the book we have explored the identity, work, death, and resurrection of Jesus. The whole point is that we cannot think of New Testament theology without considering Jesus who pointed to God. In this chapter, in light of what we have explored in terms of New Testament theology, we will deal with some contemporary issues facing us today.

COMMUNITY

Jesus breaks the traditional boundary of community and eats with sinners and tax-collectors. Jesus says, "Whoever does the will of God is my brother and sister and mother" (Mark 3:35; cf. Matt 12:50; Luke 8:21). Jesus goes beyond the traditional family and forms a God-centered new family in which sinners and tax-collectors are embraced without conditions. In this new family, those who do the work of God are truly children of God. Jesus' God is impartial and sends rain on the good and evil at the same time. In the notion of Jesus' community, enemies are also included. He also extends and changes the concept of neighbor as we see in the parable of the

Samaritan (Luke 10:25–37). In this parable, Jesus shifts the lawyer's question of "who is my neighbor?" to "who is a neighbor to a person in need?" That is, Jesus seems to say, "neighbors are not special people who deserve your care; therefore, do not be concerned about who are there. See what they need. You can become a neighbor." This means that we can all become neighbors when we take care of each other.

Likewise, Paul continues Jesus' vision of such a radical community and says that "in Christ there is no longer Jew or Gentile, free or slave or male and female" (Gal 3:28).[1] His call from God is to proclaim God's good news to the Gentile and ultimately to embrace both Jew and Gentile in the household of God. His mission program is not based on an "either/or" strategy that God chooses either Jews or Gentiles. More surprisingly, Paul sums up the whole law in a single commandment, "You shall love your neighbor as yourself" (Gal 5:14), unlike Jesus who summarizes the law and the prophets with a twofold commandment. Paul's emphasis here is that your love of neighbor completes the requirements of the law. If someone loves his or her neighbor, there is a true love of God and love of the self too. Love of neighbor cannot be separated from the love of God and the self.

Jesus and Paul re-imagined the household of God based on God's perspective that all beings and things in his creation are precious. Therefore, we have to consider all human families as God's people. Even though some do not behave as worthy of God's call, they are still children of God. Judgment is not ours, but love is.

"THE BODY OF CHRIST" (*SOMA CHRISTOU*)

It is my regret that "the body of Christ" as a metaphor in Paul's letters has been read for so long through the lens of a metaphorical organism, which results in ignoring the importance of Christ's bodily work for embodying God's gospel (good news). It is in Deutero-Pauline letters (for example, Col 1:18 or Eph 1:22–24) that "the body of Christ" is clearly used as an organism metaphor, the body of Christ as the church. But in the undisputed letters of Paul, "the body of Christ" is never put side by side with the church. Whenever Paul refers to the church, he uses the phrase "the

---

1. We should not take the stance of conservative community shown in the household codes (Col 3:18—4:1; Eph 5:21–6:9; Tit 2:1–10; 1 Pet 2:18—3:7). There, for example, women are relegated to domestic work and prohibited from taking the leadership role in the church (1 Tim 2:11–15).

church of God" (1 Cor 1:2; 10:32; 11:22; 15:9; 2 Cor 1:1; Gal 1:13), not "the church of Christ." This is because in Paul's theology, God is the owner of the church, and Christ is the foundation of the church because of his faithful obedience to God.

Accordingly, for Paul, "the body of Christ" is also primarily understood as Christ's own body—his crucifixion and his broken body because of his love of God and the world. For example, in Rom 7:4, Jesus' followers have to die to the law (of sin) through "the body of Christ" which is Christ's crucifixion. In 1 Cor 11:24, the bread represents Jesus' body and sacrifice. In 1 Cor 6:15–20, Jesus' followers have to glorify God in their bodies because they constitute parts (*mele*) of Christ, as Paul says, "Do you not know that your bodies are members of Christ?" (1 Cor 6:15). Here "members" should not be taken as the members of a community because, as we saw in 1 Cor 6:15–20, "the body of Christ" may be understood as Christ's own body, re-imagined through Christ's crucifixion. Unlike the Stoic concept of the body in the Roman Empire, Paul envisions a radical egalitarian community of all as he discusses in 1 Cor 12:12–26. Then he boils it down to a concluding statement in 12:27 and says that the Corinthian members have to embody Christ to stay in such a loving community of all. Paul says that "you are Christ-like (Christic) body," which is an attributive genitive.[2] The point is that the Corinthian members have to live a worthy life before Christ as if they constituted his body parts. Paul emphasizes holism of the members of the Corinthian church by saying they cannot live apart from Christ's sacrifice.[3]

When this very body of Christ is predicated with Jesus' followers ("You are Christ's body" in 1 Cor 12:27), the meaning of the body of Christ is now articulated in terms of the ethics of Jesus' followers. If the Corinthian readers hear they are associated with Christ's broken body, they would probably be perplexed or confused because, as 1 Cor 4:10–13 hints, some Corinthians claim that they are wise in Christ and their salvation is complete because of Christ's death. But if they correctly interpret what Paul means here, that is he suggests they imitate Christ (1 Cor 4:16; 11:1), then they are to live like Christ—a living of his body: "You are Christic body."

This new reading of "the body of Christ" metaphor challenges us to rethink who we are as Christians. What would be our knee-jerk reaction if we are identified with the body broken like Christ and thus with many bodies

2. Kim, *Christ's Body in Corinth*.

3. Kim, "Reclaiming Christ's Body," 27, 29. See also, "'Imitators' (*Mimetai*)," 147–70.

suffering today? If Christ shows his faith until he dies because of the love of God (God's righteousness), what should be our tasks as Jesus' followers?

"IN CHRIST" (*EN CHRISTO*)

The famous Pauline phrase "in Christ" (*en christo*) has been read primarily through a boundary marker in the sense that it connotes a kind of special privilege in Christ.[4] So much so that it served as a boundary marker that separated church people from non-church people.[5] The implication is that outsiders of the church are not the children of God. But this kind of boundary marking does not seem to be Paul's. For example, "in Christ" in Gal 3:28 is more than membership; it means Jesus' followers' commitment to Christ-like life. When they follow Christ's way of life, they can maintain a radical community of equality. Understood this way, "in Christ" is a

---

4. For example, in 1 Corinthians we see the following: 1:2 (those who are sanctified in Christ Jesus); 1:4 (God's grace in Christ Jesus); 1:30 (Christ is the source of our life in Christ Jesus: wisdom, righteousness, sanctification and redemption); 3:1 (infants in Christ); 4:10 (you are wise "in Christ"); 4:15 (ten thousand guardians in Christ, but not the father); 4:17 (to remind you of my ways in Christ Jesus); 15:18 (those who have died in Christ have perished); 15:19 (If for this life only we have hoped in Christ); 15:22 (For as all die in Adam, so all will be made alive in Christ); 15:31 (I die every day! That is as certain, brothers and sisters, as my boasting of you—a boast that I make in Christ Jesus our Lord; 16:24 (My love be with all of you in Christ Jesus).

5. See Dodd, *Epistle of Paul to the Romans*, 87. Dodd equates "to be baptized" with "to be in Christ." To be in Christ is to be in the church and to be in the body of Christ. Proper documentation is almost impossible to list scholars of this interpretation. A typical case of this boundary marker can be found in 1 Cor 7:39 "in the Lord" that a majority of scholars interpret *mono en kyrion* as a widow's remarrying a fellow Christian only. Likewise, the NIV translation supports it explicitly: "A woman is bound to her husband as long as he lives. But if her husband dies, she is free to marry anyone she wishes, but he must belong to the Lord." Among these interpreters are Tertullian, *Against Marcion*, 5.7; Cyprian, *Testimony*, 3.62; Jerome, *Epistles*, 123.5; Calvin, *First Epistle*, 168. Among modern scholars, Raymond Collins goes one-step further to argue for a culturally consistent marriage of endogamy in the Greco-Roman or Jewish society. See Collins, *First Corinthians*, 303. However, a small minority insists that she needs only to stay with the community not forgetting her Christian duties. For example, see Lightfoot, *Notes on the Epistles of Paul*, 225. Gordon Fee adds to this tradition: ". . . one's life comes under the eschatological view of existence outlined in vv. 29–31. Such a woman . . . from such a radically different perspective and value system from that of a pagan husband that a mixed marriage, where two becomes one, is simply unthinkable." See Fee, *First Epistle to the Corinthians*, 356. However, my opinion goes against Fee because 7.12–14 suggests that Paul does not have a negative view about a mixed marriage. In fact, Paul believes the believer-spouse will affect the sanctification of an unbeliever-spouse.

modal dative that indicates Jesus' followers' way of life.[6] If Jesus' followers walk the way of Jesus, they are in Christ. In this sense, membership (space) and a way of life (attitude) cannot be detached from each other. In fact, in Paul's letters and his theology we can hardly separate the indicative mood ("you are saved now; you are children of God") from the imperative mood ("therefore, act accordingly worthy of God's children"). Paul believes that "all who are led by the Spirit of God are children of God" (Rom 8:14). In other words, membership in God's church requires being led by the Spirit, not by a particular belief or action. Those who are led by the Spirit put to death the deeds of the body (Rom 8:13).

Paul's opponents in Corinth insist that their salvation is complete because they are wise in Christ (1 Cor 4:10–16). Interestingly, these "wise" people are passionate about the unity of the community in their own ways.[7] But Paul says they are wrong because salvation and suffering is not yet complete and repudiates this claim because they take pride in their membership and glory without participating in Christ's death. Paul's response is the Christ crucified, who is the foundation of the church. Membership in Christ without living out Christ is hollow.[8]

CHRISTIAN IDENTITY AND PLURALISM

Today we live in a very different world because of the internet and social media. The world is traveling faster than ever before, and more people entertain many different cultures or lifestyles. This is a phenomenon of postmodern culture in that pluralism is a part of it. There is a great sense of solidarity and oneness among different peoples. There is no one center or one absolute truth in the world any more. There are multiple centers that

6. Kim, *Christ's Body in Corinth*, 33–38.

7. The ideology of unity often takes a form of unitary or unilateral imposition. For the concept or the role of ideology in contemporary society and culture see Althusser, *Essays on Ideology*; and see Thomson, *Ideology and Modern Culture*, 58: "the ways in which the meaning mobilized by symbolic forms serves to establish and sustain relations of domination: to establish, in the sense that meaning may actively create and institute relations of domination; to sustain in the sense that meaning may serve to maintain and reproduce relations of domination through the ongoing process of producing and receiving symbolic forms." There is no pure, objective unity but an ideological unity. In fact, the question is about whose unity: western unity or melting into western culture or western Paul. See also Butting, "Pauline Variations on Genesis 2.24" 79–90.

8. See Sechrest, "Identity and the Embodiment of Privilege," 9–30.

coexist with constant negotiations with each other. The one universe theory is no longer accepted by scientists. We simply do not know how big the universe (or many universes) is.

How can we live in this ever-changing and challenging world of pluralism or postmodernism? Pluralism should not be taken as promoting an irresponsible relativism in the sense of "anything goes." World religions and their practices must be checked with a set of agreeable criteria. For example, the criteria should include the promotion of world peace, justice, solidarity, and well-being here and now. No one religion can replace the rest of the religions.

Christianity is not an exclusive religion if we rightly understand the Jesus who emphasizes the love of God and the love of neighbor. Jesus talks about universal ethics of love in which all people are included. As opposed to the popular belief, even the "I am" sayings of Jesus in John's Gospel cannot be read as exclusive statements.[9] For example, "I am the way" means Jesus' embodiment of God's *Logos* in a hostile world. Jesus finishes his work given by God and says "all is finished" (John 19:30). He did not finish all works such that there is nothing left for us to do for salvation. In John, Jesus always makes it clear that he is doing the works of God, which is to testify to the truth of God: God, not human masters, is love and righteousness. In this pluralistic culture, the Christian task is not to judge others or to purify the tradition or to keep doctrines but to show God's good news by engaging in the world as children of God.

RESURRECTION AND HOPE

There are two kinds of hope with which we are concerned: hope in the here and now, and hope beyond this world. Actually, the resurrection accounts in the New Testament deal with both aspects of hope: (1) resurrection as a metaphor for God's victory against evil, which emphasizes the importance or value of life here, and (2) resurrection as a mysterious real presence of the Spirit.

Even with the two aspects of hope in the New Testament, we can hardly rest because we are in the midst of all kinds of injustices and sufferings in this world. God's justice or power is hardly seen in the world today. Though we believe that the resurrection of Jesus is God's victory, there is a long overdue question about theodicy: Where is God's justice in the world?

9. Kim, *Truth, Testimony, and Transformation.*

Should Christians simply wait for the return of Jesus on the last day? Then what about all the horrendous evil and injustice done in the world now? Until then, does God delay judgment and stop doing justice in the world? If resurrection is understood only through future terms, why should we believe it or why does it matter at all since we are suffering now? Suffering or pain can hardly be justified because it is rewarded in the future. So it is not an accident that Jesus in the Fourth Gospel argues that resurrection is a present reality or relationship with God. Jesus does not say we have to endure and wait for the resurrection in the future. Rather, he says "I am the resurrection." Through his words and deeds, the quality of life can be restored if people dwell in the light. That is a new life, which must begin in the here and now. That is eternal life in the Fourth Gospel; it is a metaphor that refers to one's permanent relationship with God. Eternal life is possible by abiding in God's word of truth. Truth-living and truth-testifying is the way of life through which we can live forever. Jesus asserts that "If you continue in my word, you are truly my disciples" (John 8:31). Here Jesus' "word" is to deliver God's word of truth to his disciples and his mission is to testify to God's truth (John 18:37): "I was born and came into the world for this reason: to testify to the truth. Whoever accepts the truth listens to my voice." Then what happens? Jesus says that "you will know the truth, and the truth will make you free" (John 8:32). Even in the face of a mixture of darkness and light in the world, we can choose light and dwell in it. We can choose to fight for freedom and justice. Then God is with us now. The Spirit (the Advocate) comes to help us to testify to the truth. That is the basis of our hope. Our hope is we can now live the eternal life. Paul agrees to this when he says that "Christ was crucified by weakness, but lives by the power of God" (2 Cor 13:4). Jesus' resurrection is not merely a past event but an ongoing power of God.

In the end, we need to rethink our life and resurrection. Paul says that Jesus became a life-giving spirit. This is not reincarnation. In fact, spiritual resurrection is attested in the Gospels. Jesus' resurrection is not confirmed by his appearance (even though there are a few occasions that Jesus shows his wounds and marks of the cross's nails, this is the Evangelists' interest in making people believe in Jesus' resurrection), but by the voice of Jesus (in John 20:15–23) or by the particular deeds of Jesus (eating with the disciples in Luke 24:13–35; John 21:1–11). All this suggests that Jesus is not recognized by his appearance but through particular acts that the disciples recall.

ECOLOGY AND NEW CREATION

We are exposed to all kinds of pollution and diseases. Nature suffers be-cause of human greed. Rivers are dug deep or blocked in order for profit. Several animals are now extinct and will continue to disappear. These things negatively affect our daily lives. Thus, we also need to revisit our view of earth and "new creation" in the New Testament. First, we have to reaffirm that this world is God's creation that cannot be replaced with any-thing or exploited by us.[10] We are charged with taking care of this world, not manipulating it for our interests.

There is no hint even in the creation story, of humans being made su-perior to all other creatures or things. Humans are part of creation, not the center.[11] Each day of creation God said it was good. Heavens, earth, seas, animals, plants and trees, and humans likewise, all are created for a good purpose. All creation therefore exists harmoniously; there is no hierarchy among humans and other creatures or matters created by God. The ideal poetic image we get from Gen 1 is a story of peace and inter-relationships. Humans are created last because they depend on the previously created matter. In this creation story, humans are not self-sufficient. Earth produces various foods for them, and heaven sends the rain and wind necessary for farming. They are blessed to live in such a beautiful garden on earth. Their place in the world is not the expression of power or control, but of gratitude and humility because they are dependent on other parts of creation.

The other image we get from this beautiful creation story in Gen 1 is that humans, as the last-born creature, have to learn from God's creation. Heaven teaches them how to be impartial. The rain and light come from above (heaven) and provide all nature with necessary water and light. Earth teaches them how to be calm. It sustains numerous lives, trees and plants, animals and humans, with calmness and consistency. The point is that hu-mans in creation must be rightly understood, and we have to live together with other partners in creation, learning how to co-exist. In that sense, na-ture is a teacher or a nurturer for us, not the student whom we teach. What this further teaches us is that we need to return to a simpler life.

From the Fourth Gospel as well, we learn that this world is important and the place that God loves (John 3:16). This world is not a transient place

10. Hiebert, *Yahwist's Landscape*.

11. Though Ps 8:3–8 states humans' superiority over the created order or human creation in Gen 1 can be understood as the crown of God's creation, my argument about human dependence on creation makes a lot of sense.

that we have to escape as soon as possible. Therefore, we have to take care of it because people have to continue to live here after us. Because God loves the world, he sends Jesus to let people know about that. When Jesus departs from the world, he prays to the Father: "I am not asking you to take them out of the world, but I ask you to protect them from the evil one" (John 17:15). In this prayer, Jesus does not want them to leave the world as soon as possible because the world is hostile. Rather, Jesus wants God to protect them when they do the works of God, which is to bring light and life to the world. The need for light and life is not restricted to humans, but also to the world at large. If Jesus had prayed otherwise, he would have been a Gnostic Jesus who would have wanted to lead them to heaven as soon as possible. But Jesus asks, "Sanctify them in the truth; your word is truth" (John 17:17). Jesus sends the disciples into the world so that they may continue his work in the here and now. So this world is the mission field to which we have to minister. This world must be God's redemptive place and we have to work with God to make that happen.

The language of new creation or the apocalyptic language in the Bible should be corrected. A popular reading of that language is based on the assumption that the new world (New Jerusalem in Revelation or the end of the day in the Gospels or in Paul's letters) is established only after the current one is destroyed. This new world requires a catastrophic end to the current world. Often, popular end-of-the-world movies are greatly pessimistic to such a degree that the new world is unlike the current one. This is a typical view of an apocalypse shared in first-century Palestine.

But there is also another view that does not require such utter destruction of the current world to bring in a new one. As Crossan argues, the ancient prophets in the Hebrew Bible hold such a view that the apocalyptic words and visions point to a new world of renewal with new orders and systems in place.[12] Also, Crossan thinks Jesus' proclamation of God's kingdom must be rooted in the here and now. This kind of eschatology is called "permanent eschatology" or "prophetic eschatology," which means "the permanence of God as the one who challenges world and shatters its complacency repeatedly."[13] In a way, what is destroyed is not nature or hardware but software or the

---

12. Crossan lists five views of eschatology: consequent eschatology (A. Schweitzer); realized eschatology (C. H. Dodd); progressive eschatology (J. Jeremias); and permanent eschatology (Crossan). See Crossan, *In Parables*, 23–26. See also A. Schweitzer, *Quest of the Historical Jesus*, 356; Dodd, *Parables of the Kingdom*, 82–84; Jeremias, *Parables of Jesus*, 230.

13. Crossan, *In Parables*, 26.

status quo. If we take this view of prophetic eschatology, this world is not going to be destroyed and, thus, it must be protected as God's creation.

Accordingly, Paul's language of new creation in Rom 8:19–23; 2 Cor 5:17; and Gal 6:15 should be understood as supporting the preservation of the earth and environment, not as replacing the current one with a new one, as often imagined by a future-oriented apocalyptic drama wherein God destroys all the current natural environments and systems and makes a new heaven and earth. In Romans 8 we hear Paul emphasizing that creation also suffers because of human sin that turns creation into the object of control or worship. Paul says, "the whole creation has been groaning in labor pains until now" (Rom 8:22). So the solution is "the creation waits with eager longing for the revealing of the children of God" (Rom 8:19). If the children of God are in a good relationship with their God, "the creation itself will be set free from its bondage to decay and will obtain the freedom of the glory of the children of God" (Rom 8:21).

Likewise, in 2 Cor 5:17 ("So if anyone is in Christ, there is a new creation: everything old has passed away; see, everything has become new!"), Paul says that once we are up to Christ-like life, we are anew in our relationship with God; that is, a new creation, a new community in Christ, seeking God's righteousness, which concerns all living and non-living in the world. Though here "a new creation" does not directly refer to the creation as in Romans, a new Christian life must have a good relationship with the earth because it is God's creation.

In a similar vein, Gal 6:15 ("For neither circumcision nor uncircumcision is anything; but a new creation is everything!") also supports the view of 2 Cor 5:17, though in this context the issue has to do with a Jewish version of the gospel. "A new creation" here means a new identity in Christ, not based on ethnicity or laws, but based on God's impartial love that is shown through Christ's faithful obedience and through those who participate in his faith. Though a new creation here is not the same thing as the creation in Romans, again the inferring question is: How can Christians become a new creation while the earth suffers? If they are in peace with God and neighbor, they must also be with the earth because it is God's creation in which the divine nature is revealed according to Rom 1:20–23. Paul does not specify what is revealed in nature. Perhaps Lao-tzu, a fourth-century BCE philosopher in China, author of the *Tao Te Ching*, may help us understand the rule and role of nature in our lives. Here I read his work from the perspective of a biblical scholar.[14] I find both the *Tao Te Ching* (*Dao De Jing*) and the Bible have a lot in common in terms of an ideal lifestyle that must embody nature. Lao-tzu writes a practical yet critical wisdom that proposes an alternative way of life rooted in nature. In seeking practical wisdom, Lao-tzu asks people to return to the way in nature, not in the sense of a person's withdrawal from everyday life but in ways that people rethink the meaning of life, moving away from self-seeking powers and glory, self-edifying pleasures, and the attitude of ignoring others. The language of the *Tao Te Ching* is certainly paradoxical and deconstructive. Lao-tzu dreams of a world of peace and justice and advises that people be like water or be one with dust. As we know a tree by its fruit, the person following the way of nature produces good fruit. It is like Jesus' sayings that emphasize the importance of sacrifice: "For whoever would save his life will lose it; and whoever loses his life for my sake, he will save it" (Luke 9:24; cf. Mark 8:35—9:1; Matt 10:39); "Unless a grain of wheat falls into the earth and dies, it remains alone; but if it dies, it bears much fruit" (John 12:24).

CONCLUDING REMARKS

Life is both a gift and predicament. This kind of sheer realization that we humans are not self-sufficient enables us to be humble and feel a sense of solidarity with other beings and creation in the world. Indeed, nothing can exist in isolation. If this is the concept of religion, the New Testament writings and Jesus, as I have shown, give us a plethora of religious insights and challenges to consider as we live in this world. Jesus lived as best as he could to urge the people that they must honor God and his creation, while respecting others and protecting the weak.

As a house built on sand falls, a theology or ethics without a good foundation is sure to fall. In this book, I tried to address the problem of a shaky, individualistic theology through a critical reexamination of Jesus' life and work. Jesus radically interpreted the law and the prophets in relation to God's kingly rule in the here and now. This Jesus was remembered by his followers and claimed as the Messiah. Jesus finished the work that he was supposed to do, and now it is his followers who have to continue his work. This is where the story of Jesus of Nazareth and the significance of his life and work converge. Ultimately, New Testament theology needs to be endlessly embodied and rewritten by those who participate in God's work through the Messiah.

14. For more see Kim, *Why Christians Need to Read the Tao Te Ching*.

Bibliography

Adam, A. K. M. *Making Sense of New Testament Theology: "Modern" Problems and Prospects*. Macon, GA: Mercer University Press, 1995.

Althusser, Louis. *Essays on Ideology*. London: Verso, 1984.

Armstrong, Karen. *The Case for God*. New York: Anchor, 2009.

Ashton, John. "History and Theology in New Testament Studies." In *The Nature of New Testament Theology*, edited by Christopher Rowland and Christopher Tuckett, 1–17. Malden, MA: Blackwell, 2006.

Bailey, Lloyd R. Sr. *Biblical Perspectives on Death*. Philadelphia: Fortress, 1981.

Barnes, Michael. *In the Presence of Mystery*. Mystic, CT: Twenty-third, 2003.

Bella, Peter. *Challenges to New Testament Theology: An Attempt to Justify the Enterprise*. Peabody, MA: Hendrickson, 1997.

Borg, Marcus. "A Chronological NT." *Huffington Post*. August 3, 2012. http://www.huffingtonpost.com/marcus-borg/a-chronological-new-testament_b_1823018.html.

———. *Jesus: A New Vision*. New York: HarperOne, 1991.

Borg, Marcus, and N. T. Wright. *The Meaning of Jesus: Two Visions*. New York: HarperOne, 1999.

Brown, Raymond. *The Birth of the Messiah: A Commentary on the Infancy Narratives in the Gospels of Matthew and Luke*. New Haven, CT: Yale University Press, 1999.

———. *The Death of the Messiah*. New Haven, CT: Yale University Press, 1998.

Bultmann, R. "Die Frage nach dem messianischen Bewusstsein Jesus und das Petrusbekennnis." *Zeitschrift für die neutestamentliche Wissenschaft* 19 (1919/20) 165–74.

———. "The Primitive Christian Kerygma and the Historical Jesus." In *The Historical Jesus and the Kerygmatic Christ: Essays on the New Quest of the Historical Jesus*, edited by C. E. Braaten and R. A. Harrisville, 15–53. Nashville: Abingdon, 1964.

———. *Theology of the New Testament*. Translated by Kendrick Grobel. New York: Scribners, 1951.

Butting, Klara. "Pauline Variations on Genesis 2.24: Speaking of the Body of Christ in the context of the Discussion of Lifestyles." *Journal for the Study of the New Testament* 79 (2000) 79–90.

Caird, G. B. *New Testament Theology*. Edited by L. D. Hurst. Oxford: Oxford University Press, 1994.

Bibliography

Calvin, John. *First Epistle of Paul to the Corinthians*. Grand Rapids: Eerdmans, 1996.

Campbell, Cynthia. *A Multitude of Blessings*. Louisville, KY: WJKP, 2007.

Cartlidge, David, and David Dungan, eds. *Documents for the Study of the Gospels*. Minneapolis, MN: Fortress, 1994.

Charlesworth, James. *The Historical Jesus*. Nashville: Abingdon, 2008.

———. *Jesus within Judaism*. New York: Doubleday, 1988.

Collins, John. *Commentary on the Book of Daniel*. Minneapolis: Fortress, 1993.

———. "Pre-Christian Jewish Messianism." In *The Messiah in Early Judaism and Christianity*, edited by Magnus Zetterholm, 1–20. Minneapolis, MN: Fortress, 2002.

Collins, Raymond. *First Corinthians*. Collegeville, MN: Liturgical, 1999.

Crossan, John. *The Birth of Christianity*. San Francisco: HarperSanFrancisco, 1998.

———. *Excavating Jesus: Beneath the Stones, Behind the Texts*. San Francisco: HarperSanFrancisco, 2002.

———. *The Historical Jesus: The Life of a Mediterranean Jewish Peasant*. San Francisco: HarperSanFrancisco, 1991.

———. *Jesus: A Revolutionary Biography*. New York: HarperCollins, 1995.

———. "The Message of Jesus." In *The Message of Jesus: John Dominic Crossan and Ben Witherington III in Dialogue*, edited by Robert Stewart, 1–31. Minneapolis, MN: Fortress, 2013.

———. *In Parables: The Challenge of the Historical Jesus*. Sonoma, CA: Polebridge, 1992.

———. "The Resurrection." In *The Resurrection of Jesus: John Dominic Crossan and N.T. Wright in Dialogue*, edited by Robert Stewart, 23–44. Minneapolis, MN: Fortress, 2006.

Culpepper, R. Alan. "Contours of the Historical Jesus." In *The Quest for the Real Jesus*, edited by Jan Van der Watt. Leiden: Brill, 2013.

Dodd, C. H. *The Epistle of Paul to the Romans*. New York: R. Long & R. R. Smith, 1932.

———. *The Parables of the Kingdom*. New York: Scribner, 1961.

Dowd, Shary, and Elizabeth Malbon. "The Significance of Jesus' Death in Mark: Narrative Context and Authorial Audience." *Journal of Biblical Literature* 125.2 (2006) 271–97.

Dunn, James D. G. *Jesus Remembered: Christianity in the Making*. Vol. 1. Grand Rapids: Eerdmans, 2003.

———. *The Oral Gospel Tradition*. Grand Rapids: Eerdmans, 2013.

Ehrman, Bart. *Misquoting Jesus*. New York: HarperCollins, 2005.

———. *New Testament*. 5th ed. New York: Oxford University Press, 2012.

Fee, Gordon. *The First Epistle to the Corinthians*. Grand Rapids: Eerdmans, 1987.

Feldman, Louis H. *Josephus and Modern Scholarship, 1937–1980*. Berlin: de Gruyter, 1984.

Fredriksen, P. *Jesus of Nazareth, King of the Jews: A Jewish Life and the Emergence of Christianity*. New York: Alfred A. Knopf, 2000.

Frei, Hans W. *The Identity of Jesus Christ*. Philadelphia: Fortress, 1975.

Freyne, Sean. *Jesus, a Jewish Galilean*. London: T. & T. Clark, 2005.

Gaventa, Beverly, and Richard Hays, eds. *Seeking the Identity of Jesus: A Pilgrimage*. Grand Rapids: Eerdmans, 2008.

Gillman, Neil. *The Death of Death: Resurrection and Immortality in Jewish Thought*. Woodstock, VT: Jewish Lights, 1997.

Gossai, Hemchand. *Social Critique by Israel's Eighth-Century Prophets: Justice and Righteousness in Context*. Eugene, OR: Wipf & Stock, 1993.

Grant, Michael. *Jesus: An Historian's Review of the Gospels*. New York: Scribner, 1977.

Hanson K. C., and Douglas Oakman. *Palestine in the Time of Jesus: Social Structures and Social Conflicts*. Minneapolis, MN: Fortress, 2002.

Hiebert, Ted. "The Tower of Babel and the Origin of the World's Cultures." *Journal of Biblical Literature* 126.1 (2007) 29–58.

———. *The Yahwist's Landscape: Nature and Religion in Early Israel*. Minneapolis, MN: Fortress, 1996.

Holtzman, H. J. *Lehrbuch neutestamentlichen Theologie*. 2 vols. Tübingen: Mohr, 1911.

———. "Das leere Grab und die gegenwärtigen Verhandlungen über die Auferstehung Jesu." In *Theologische Rundschau*, vol. 9, edited by Wilhelm Bousset and Rudolf Bultmann, 79–86. Tübingen: Mohr Siebeck, 1906.

Horsley, Richard. *Archaeology, History, and Society in Galilee: The Social Context of Jesus and the Rabbis*. London: T. & T. Clark, 1996.

———. *Jesus and Empire*. Minneapolis, MN: Fortress, 2003.

Jeremias, J. *The Parables of Jesus*. New York: Scribner, 1963.

Johnson, Luke T. "Does a Theology of the Canonical Gospels Make Sense?" In *The Nature of New Testament Theology*, edited by Christopher Rowland and Christopher Tuckett, 93–108. Malden, MA: Blackwell, 2006.

Josephus. "Testimonium Flavianum: Josephus' Reference to Jesus." *Early Christian Writings*. http://www.earlychristianwritings.com/testimonium.html.

Kähler, M. *The So-called Historical Jesus and the Historic, Biblical Christ*. Translated and edited by C. E. Braaten. Philadelphia: Fortress, 1988.

Käsemann, Ernst. "The Problem of the Historical Jesus." In *Essays on New Testament Themes*. Studies in Biblical Theology 41. London: SCM, 1964.

Kim, Yung Suk. *Biblical Interpretation: Theory, Process, and Criteria*. Eugene, OR: Pickwick, 2013.

———. *Christ's Body in Corinth*. Minneapolis, MN: Fortress, 2008.

———. "'Imitators' (*Mimetai*) in 1 Cor. 4:16 and 11:1: A New Reading of Threefold Embodiment." *Horizons in Biblical Theology* 33 (2011) 147–70.

———. "Jesus' Death in Context." *Living Pulpit* 16.2 (2007) 12–13.

———. "*Lex Talionis* in Exod 21:22–25: Its Origin and Context." In *Perspectives on Hebrew Scriptures* III, edited by Ehud Ben Zvi, 99–112. Piscataway, NJ: Gorgias, 2007.

———. "Reclaiming Christ's Body (*soma christou*): Embodiment of God's Gospel in Paul's Letters." *Interpretation* 67.1 (2013) 20–29.

———. *Theological Introduction to Paul's Letters: Exploring a Threefold Theology of Paul*. Eugene, OR: Cascade, 2011.

———. *Truth, Testimony, and Transformation*. Eugene, OR: Cascade, 2014.

———. *Why Christians Need to Read the Tao Te Ching*. Charleston, SC: Createspace, 2014.

Klausner, J. *Jesus of Nazareth*, London: Macmillan, 1925.

Kloppenborg, John S. *Q the Earliest Gospel*. Louisville, KY: WJKP, 2008.

Knight, Douglas A. "Ethics and Human Life in the Hebrew Bible." In *Justice and the Holy*, edited by Douglas A. Knight and Peter J. Paris. Atlanta, GA: Scholars, 1989.

Le Donne, Anthony. *Historical Jesus: What Can We Know and How Can We Know It?* Grand Rapids: Eerdmans, 2011.

Lightfoot, J. B. *Notes on the Epistles of Paul*. Grand Rapids: Baker, 1980.

Lightfoot, Neil. *How We Got the Bible*. Grand Rapids: Baker, 2003.

Lüdemann, G. *The Resurrection of Christ: A Historical Inquiry*. Amherst, NY: Prometheous, 2004.

Bibliography

Mafico, Temba. "Just, Justice." *Anchor Bible Dictionary*, edited by David Freedman, 3:1127–29. New York: Doubleday, 1992.

———. *Yahweh's Emergence as "Judge" Among the Gods: A Study of the Hebrew Root Špt.* Lewiston, NY: Edwin Mellen, 2006.

Marshall, I. Howard. *A Concise New Testament Theology*. Downers Grove, IL: InterVarsity, 2008.

Marxsen, Willi. *The Resurrection of Jesus of Nazareth*. Philadelphia: Fortress, 1970.

Matera, Frank J. *New Testament Theology: Exploring Diversity and Unity*. Louisville, KY: WJKP, 2007.

McIver, Robert. *Jesus, Memory, and the Gospels*. Atlanta, GA: SBL, 2011.

Meggitt, Justin. "Psychology and the Historical Jesus." In *Jesus and Psychology* edited by Fraser Watts. West Conshohocken, PA: Temple Foundation, 2007.

Meier, John. *A Marginal Jew: Rethinking the Historical Jesus*. New York: Doubleday, 1991.

Miller, John. *Jesus at Thirty*. Minneapolis, MN: Fortress, 1997.

Miller, Robert J. "The Illegitimacy of Jesus in the Gospel of Matthew." *Juniata Voices* 8 (2008) 24–36.

Morgan, Robert. "New Testament Theology Since Bultmann." *Expository Times* 119.10 (2008) 472–80.

Moxnes, Halvor. "Identity in Jesus' Galilee—From Ethnicity to Locative Intersectionality." *Biblical Interpretation* 18 (2010) 390–416.

Oakman, Douglas. *The Political Aims of Jesus*. Minneapolis, MN: Fortress, 2012.

O'Day, Gail. "John." In *The New Interpreter's Study Bible*, edited by Walter Harrelson, 1905–51. Nashville: Abingdon, 2003.

Pannenberg, Wolfhart. *Basic Questions in Theology*. Philadelphia, PA: Westminster, 1969.

———. *Jesus: God and Man*. Philadelphia, PA: Westminster, 1968.

———. *Revelation as History*. New York: Macmillian, 1969.

———. *Systematic Theology. Vol. 2*. Translated by W. Bromiley. Grand Rapids: Eerdmans, 2013.

Paulus, H. E. G. *Das Leben Jesu als Grundlage einer Geschichte des Urchristentums*. Heidelberg: Winter, 1828.

Peppard, Michael. *The Son of God in the Roman World: Divine Sonship in its Social and Political Context*. New York: Oxford University Press, 2011.

Räissänen, Heikki. *Beyond New Testament Theology: A Story and a Program*. Philadelphia: Trinity, 2000.

Reed, Jonathan, and J. D. Crossan. *Excavating Jesus*. New York: HarperOne, 2001.

Reinhartz, Adele. "The Temple Cleansing and the Death of Jesus." In *Purity, Holiness, and Identity in Judaism and Christianity*, edited by Carl Ehrlich, 101–11. Tübingen: Mohr Siebeck, 2013.

Said, Edward. *Humanism and Democratic Criticism*. New York: Columbia University Press, 2004.

Sanders, E. P. *The Historical Figure of Jesus*. London: Penguin, 1993.

Schaberg, Jane. *The Illegitimacy of Jesus: A Feminist Theological Interpretation of the Infancy Narratives*. San Francisco: Harper & Row, 1987.

Schreiner, Thomas. *Magnifying God in Christ: A Summary of New Testament Theology*. Grand Rapids: Baker, 2010.

Sechrest, Love. "Identity and the Embodiment of Privilege in Corinth." In *1 and 2 Corinthians*, edited by Yung Suk Kim, 9–30. Minneapolis, MN: Fortress, 2013.

Schweitzer, A. *The Quest of the Historical Jesus*. New York: Macmillan, 1968.

Shillington, V. George. *Jesus and Paul before Christianity: Their World and Work in Retrospect*. Eugene, OR: Cascade, 2011.

Smith, Daniel. *The Post-Mortem Vindication of Jesus in the Sayings Gospel Q*. London: T. & T. Clark, 2007.

———. "Revisiting the Empty Tomb: The Post-Mortem Vindication of Jesus in Mark and Q." *Novum Testamentum* 45.2 (2003) 123–37.

Smith, Huston. *Why Religion Matters: The Fate of the Human Spirit in an Age of Disbelief*. New York: HarperCollins, 2000.

Spivey, Robert, et al. *The Anatomy of the New Testament*. 7th ed. Minneapolis, MN: Fortress, 2013.

Stanton, Graham. *The Gospels and Jesus*. 2nd ed. Oxford: Oxford University Press, 2002.

Stendahl, Krister. "The Apostle Paul and the Introspective Conscience of the West." *Harvard Theological Review* 56.3 (1963) 199–215.

———. *Paul Among Jews and Gentiles*. Philadelphia: Fortress, 1976.

Stewart, Roy A. *Rabbinic Theology*. London: Oliver and Boyd, 1961.

Strauss, D. F. *The Life of Jesus Critically Examined*. Cambridge: Cambridge University Press, 2010.

Tabor, James. "A Historical Look at the Birth of Jesus: Part 4." *Tabor Blog*. December 26, 2012. http://jamestabor.com/2012/12/26/a-historical-look-at-the-birth-of-jesus-part-4.

Theissen, Gerd, and Annette Merz. *The Historical Jesus: A Comprehensive Guide*. Minneapolis, MN: Fortress, 1998.

Thomson, John. *Ideology and Modern Culture: Critical Social Theory in the Era of Mass Communication*. Stanford, CA: Stanford University Press, 1990.

Trible, Phyllis. "The Authority of the Bible." In *New Interpreter's Study Bible*, edited by Walter Harrelson, 2243–60. Nashville: Abingdon.

Tuckett, Christopher. "Does the 'Historical Jesus' Belong Within a New Testament Theology?" In *The Nature of New Testament Theology*, edited by Christopher Rowland and Christopher Tuckett, 231–47. Malden, MA: Blackwell, 2006.

Via, Dan. *What is New Testament Theology?* Minneapolis, MN: Fortress, 2002.

Wainwright, Elain. *Shall We Look for Another: A Feminist Rereading of the Matthean Jesus*. Maryknoll, NY: Orbis, 1998.

Warrior, Robert. "Canaanites, Cowboys, and Indians: Deliverance, Conquest, and Liberation Theology Today." In *Voices from the Margin: Interpreting the Bible in the Third World*, edited by R. S. Sugirtharajah, 277–85. Maryknoll, NY: Orbis, 1995.

Weiss, Bernard. *Biblical Theology of the New Testament*. 2 vols. Edinburgh: T. & T. Clark, 1882.

Westbrook, Raymond, and Theodore J. Lewis. "Who Led the Scapegoat in Leviticus 16:21?" *Journal of Biblical Literature* 127.3 (2008) 417–22.

Westermann, Claus. *Basic Forms of Prophetic Speech*. Louisville, KY: WJKP, 1991.

Wink, Walter. *The Human Being: Jesus and the Enigma of the Son of the Man*. Minneapolis, MN: Fortress, 2001.

Witherington III, Ben. "Opening Statement." In *The Message of Jesus: John Dominic Crossan and Ben Witherington III in Dialogue*, edited by Robert Stewart. Minneapolis, MN: Fortress, 2013.

Wrede, William. *The Messianic Secret in the Gospels*. Cambridge: James Clarke, 1971.

———. "The Task and Methods of 'New Testament Theology.'" In *The Nature of New Testament Theology*, edited by Robert Morgan. Naperville, IL: Allenson, 1973.

Zeller, Dieter. "Entrückung zur Ankunft als Menschensohn." In *A cause de l'Evangile: études sur les Synoptiques et les Actes offertes au P. Jacques Dupont à l'occasion de son 70e anniversaire*, edited by Jacques Dupont, 513–30. Paris: Cerf, 1985.

Index